Robert Herzog is a writer's writer. The loneliness and longing of the father-wound is palpable throughout the book; yet he rises to remarkable levels of eloquence and compassion to discover goodness, a love of life, and forgiveness. What a son to such a father. What a father to his three sons. This book can help all of our fathers and sons bask in the mercy and healing that men and our world desire."

—RICHARD ROHR, Author and Founder of the Center for Action and Contemplation

Robert Herzog has written a beautiful book for men, about boys and masculinity, love and vulnerability, about fathers and sons. It sings in ways that men rarely do, but really should. Highly recommended.

—JON M. SWEENEY, Author of *My Life in Seventeen Books: A Literary Memoir*

Through a narrative both tender and harsh, and in language both vividly poetic and insightfully analytic, Robert Herzog's memoir confirms that the parent-child relationship does not end when the parent dies. Indeed, it reveals that even when the relationship is marked by difficulty and distance, the possibility of profound healing is always there for us—if we are willing to delve deeply into the past and also to transform our own behavior in the present and toward the future. With remarkable honesty, and laced with moments of a delightfully dark sense of humor, this memoir shares an intensely personal journey. At the same time, it transcends the personal through the writer's reflections on the ways that a complex web of factors—including place, class, history, intergenerational dynamics and our received myths and values—come together to shape who we are and what we hope for ourselves and the people we love.

—NOELLE OXENHOLDER, Author of *The Eros of Parenting*

Bury Me with the Dogs

Fathers, Sons, and an Accidental Manhood

ROBERT HERZOG

Copyright © 2024 by Robert Herzog

All rights reserved. This book or any portion thereof may not be reproduced or used in any manner whatsoever without the express written permission of the publisher except for the use of brief quotations in a book review or scholarly journal.

NO AI TRAINING: Without in any way limiting the author [and publisher's] exclusive rights under copyright, any use of this publication to "train" generative artificial intelligence (AI) technologies to generate text is expressly prohibited. The author reserves all rights to license uses of this work for generative AI training and development of machine learning language models.

Print: 978-1-958670-38-5
Ebook: 978-1-958670-37-8

Printed in the United States of America

Library of Congress Cataloguing-in-Publication Data
Bury Me With the Dogs: Fathers, Sons, and an Accidental Manhood / Robert Herzog

For my Sons, Silas, Ezra, and Arlo
Behold, the only thing greater than myself

And for my Father, John David "Herk" Herzog, Jr.
…a good man

Table of Contents

Acknowledgements xiii
Prologue 1
Chapter One 5
Chapter Two 17
Chapter Three 31
Chapter Four 39
Chapter Five 49
Chapter Six 61
Chapter Seven 69
Chapter Eight 89
Chapter Nine 103
Chapter Ten 119
Chapter Eleven 131
Chapter Twelve 143
Chapter Thirteen 161

We live in a threshold moment. We are waking up to the Earth again. We are awakening to the Feminine and the desire to faithfully tend the interrelationship of all things. In this moment, politically, culturally, and religiously, we are witnessing the death throes of a shadow form of Masculine power that has arrayed itself over against the Earth and over against the sacredness of the Feminine. This shadow form of power, however, has no ultimate future, for it is essentially false in its betrayal of the Earth and the Feminine. So in fear it is lashing out with unprecedented force. But it is not the deep spirit of this moment in time. Something else is trying to be born.

John Philip Newell
Sacred Earth, Sacred Soul

Last night as I was sleeping,
I dreamt—marvelous error!—
that I had a beehive
here inside my heart.
And the golden bees
were making white combs
and sweet honey
from my old failures.

Antonio Machado
Last Night as I Was Sleeping
Translated by Robert Bly

Acknowledgements

Well, it only took 13 years to finish the book; in that long, wayfaring time there have been legions of folks who have contributed to the process. First, I have to thank all of the nameless, noble baristas who poured me innumerable espresso shots at various coffee shops around Sonoma County while I typed earnestly at my laptop.

Thank you to the circle of men with whom I have sat for the last ten years. Thank you, Peter, Gabriel, Justin, Troy, Angel, and Rob—all of us fathers of boys and young men. I appreciate your collective wisdom and your willingness to hear my stories and to share yours. You all give me hope for building a critical mass of men to serve as Elders.

Thank you to my virtual circle of men who have endured reading early and awkward versions of this book and provided kind words, helpful critique, and the occasional cigar and glass of whiskey. Thank you, brothers from another mother, Scott, Cadmon, Jeff, Phil, Dave, Clinton, Dan, Vince, and others who have shaped the narrative while knowing me in different iterations as a boy, teenager, and a man. Thanks especially to Terry for long talks about fathers and sons and righteous road trips through West Texas and the Southwest.

I am grateful to my Editor, Noelle Oxenholder, whose suggestions for the book have been invaluable. Thank you for newly discovered friendships.

A heartfelt offering of thanks for Jonathan Foster at SacraSage for his assistance in seeing this project through to the end with remarkable wit, wisdom, and irreverent reverence.

Thank you to my mentor in men's work, Father Richard Rohr. My time at the Center for Action and Contemplation in New Mexico and during my Rite of Passage was transformative. Blessings to you, Dear Man.

A hearty thanks to the poets and scholars and authors for their compelling work—Maritn Shaw, Robert Bly, Robert Moore, Douglas Gillette, James Hillman, and Michael Meade, among numerous others. Thank you also to bell hooks, Marion Woodman, and Sophie Strand, whose books on men and masculinity are astounding.

I am profoundly grateful for the women who have joined me and challenged me on this journey of becoming a man. Especially to my teacher and herald of 10,000 joys and 10,000 sorrows, Dr. Susan Dubin. I deeply appreciate your wisdom.

To Xochi, who has mothered our boys exquisitely and travelled with me along this sublime and sometimes vexing path of partnership in all its sundry forms.

For my boys, Silas, Ezra, and Arlo—you are my most compelling teachers, you make me want to be a better man and father, and you continue to be the joys of my life as I observe your own journeys to manhood from near and far.

And finally, to my Father, John David "Herk" Herzog Jr. Thank you for showing up, for persisting, and for being a good man.

Prologue

*Take your well-disciplined strengths
and stretch them between two
opposing poles.
Because inside human beings
is where God learns.*

Rainer Marie Rilke
Just as the Winged Energy of Delight
Translated by Robert Bly

Men don't read, the prevailing opinion goes. It's an interesting fact to reconcile in writing a book about men and for men.

I read. Voraciously. I read in the safe confines of my boyhood bedroom, separating myself from the chaos of my family. I read to be alone. I read to know that I wasn't alone, taking comfort in the local newspaper's narratives of my boyhood sports heroes on the Pirates and the Steelers, longing to find the entrance to Narnia in the back of the closet at the top of the stairs, and identifying with the harrowing journeys of Frodo and Samwise.

My father read. When he died, he left behind stacks of Military Modeler magazines and Louis L'Amour novels. My mother quickly disposed of in the trash the day he died, dismissing, and dismantling her pain of memory. I imagine that he struggled with reading, having dropped out of high school, joining the Army to leave his violent alcoholic father behind, and later earning his GED while stationed in Germany during the advent of the Cold War.

I can vividly recall him sitting at the kitchen table, the small color TV blaring the local news in the haze of cigarette smoke, while he chipped away at the correspondence courses assigned to him as a nuclear missile tech to nobly protect the country and our hometown Pittsburgh from the Soviet scourge.

I would peek my crew-cut head around the corner, holding my breath so as not to break the spell of his efforts and murmuring incantations just under his breath. I was proud of him, even at a young age, intuiting somehow that he was working diligently to better himself. To provide for his family. To buttress him from the shame that was a constant threat, the barbarian at the gate who would crush his small empire.

And more frequently I was scared of him, scared of the rage that would rise from his steely silence, the shrapnel from his explosions wreaking havoc on those in the immediate blast zone. In frustration, he would occasionally throw the light-blue covered class booklet with the fine print and scientific hieroglyphics against the wall, sending the pages flying and the copper-colored fasteners under the kitchen table and into the dusty corners when his noble efforts were rebuffed after having failed the end of chapter quiz.

I knew to duck my head out of the kitchen during these moments, lest I be on the receiving end of his rage and other emotional projectiles. I would return to the scene of his crime later in the night when his two- or three-, or even six-beer buzz cajoled him into a restless sleep in the bedroom upstairs or on the living room couch. I would faithfully gather the strewn pages and put them back in numerical order, reattaching the fasteners through the stacks of three-hole punched pages of graphs and formulas and looming end of chapter exams. I would return the book to its rightful place at his seat at the kitchen table in our tightly packed sunflower- and nicotine-yellow kitchen. Like his rage had never happened. A new start, a re-do, as I conspired with the universe and the United States Army to allow him to begin again.

As I have entertained these memories while he lay dying, I persevere to remember him differently. Crawling on hands and knees on the kitchen floor, finally learning how to bow reverently in the presence of our complicated relationship, I gather those letters and words strewn about the kitchen and through my childhood. I gather them up, carefully scraping them from the wall, brushing them gently into the dustpan of memory. I rearrange them, daring to find order in the chaos.

The letters scraped off of the wall and the floor become words. The words become sentences. The sentences become paragraphs, and they congregate together to construct this love letter to him.

I long to return those words to him. That somehow, they may nourish him for his journey, providing him and me comfort from the haunting that we have both endured since he died. The haunting of fathers and sons in our family and across time in all families.

The kabbalist origin story of *Zim Zum* retells of the divine light bestowed upon humanity in earthen vessels. The dried clay is unable to bear the profound light and shatters, sending broken shards throughout the world. The task, then, of the pilgrim, of the wayfarer, is to roam and find those shards containing the Light. And return them to the Divine.

This is the concept of *tikkun olam*. Restoring the world to the Divine. Restoring dignity to my father. We restore through re-storying. Telling and retelling our stories. The events of the past do not change through our efforts, as much as we may long for them to do so. But the healing, the learning is to be found in the new meaning that we assign to those events, as we transcend the gravitational pull of the historical and rise into the realm of the eternal. Time and timelessness.

The new meaning allows me to begin again. To engage this new story while restoring the old to its rightful place.

To understand him. To remember him differently. Even daring to celebrate how he fathered me. To forgive him. To seek his forgiveness. To forgive myself for the things I said to him as he was dying.

To heal. To father my own sons differently. To father all of our sons. To remember the past. To dare to remember the future. To restore and renew the divine nature of masculinity, married to the wisdom of the divine feminine.

To understand, like Rilke implores, that it is within human beings where God learns.

To fitfully and finally realize that perhaps it is within Sons where Fathers learn.

Chapter One

*During times of peace,
sons bury their fathers.
But in times of war,
it is fathers
who send their sons to the grave.*

HERODOTUS
The Histories
Book 1, Chapter 87

I held my father's ashes in the cold gray of Pittsburgh early winter, just over the hill from the family home, honoring my father's final wish to be buried with the remains of his beloved dogs. The air was thick with expectancy of the first snow, still weeks away but the inevitable loomed somewhere over the horizon.

Grief always seems to intensify the sensory experience of the pilgrim tasked with the rituals of the dead and buried. I was tempted to taste the hard clay that rested upon the tip of the shovel. The shovel's blade rested in the cold, unforgiving ground like a makeshift Excalibur, waiting for the young boy, Arthur, to pull it from the ground to assume his rightly place upon the throne. To feel the rough and crumbling consistency of its loamy bits in the palm of my hand as callouses formed at the mercy of the wooden shovel handle.

The King is dead. Long live the King.

For now.

The line of succession from one King to the next, from Father to Son is a complicated one. It plays out in the life of the relationship between King and successor, as in myths told throughout time and more recent movie scripts and HBO series. The Father fears the Son—Chronos devours his children, Herod decrees firstborns to death, Logan Roy ridicules his ineffective heirs and potential inheritors of the Waystar-Royco fortune.

Sons long for their place on the throne. And fear just how heavy weighs that crown. Kings demand fealty and achieve it by any means necessary, often with violent shame and anger. Sons long for their rightful place as powerful potentate, while knowing that their Father's demise and ultimate death is the unfortunate means to their rise.

At times that death is anticipated and prepared for. Other times, the succession plan is thrust upon us in the teary haze of grief, fear, and regret.

I would bury him as he wished, with the remains and spirits of his dogs helping him cross the threshold into his next life, whatever afterlife awaited him. Along with the remains of those strays and purebreds two- or three-feet under, we would all bear witness to the return from domestication to wildness. From dust to dust, bone to ash.

From dog to wolf. Tame to feral. Forgetting to remembering.

From loneliness to salvage with the ancestors, calling him home, to a sense of ease and station that he had never known in his waking life. Where that ease and quiet would live in his bones, and now in the bony fragments and ash in this cold metal box.

I longed for that same ease in the marrow of my own bones while they still pulsed with life and with the blood and DNA inherited from my father and his line. The dying of a parent makes you keenly aware of your own ticking clock. Perched between roles of fatherless son and father to my own three sons.

Blood and bone.

And the memory of the past spread out before me like the multitudes of gray that mirrored the wintry sky above me—silver, ash, gunship gray, even a hint of stormy, dangerous black.

And the memory of the future, still unwritten, with that same smell of snow hanging in the air.

Fathers and sons.

They are always moving in and out of varied states of war and warring, interrupted by times of peace and precarious detente.

My father and I were no exception.

It's part of the old trope from English Composition 101, if you'll pardon the 80's patriarchal language: man versus man, man versus nature, man versus himself.

Man versus his son.

The theme has occupied our consciousness for some time now—God commanding Abraham to sacrifice his son, Isaac, while the God of the New Testament ups the ante by sacrificing his only begotten Son; the narrative sold tickets for Shakespeare; made Freud famous (and then infamous); propped up Empires; brought Empires down, much to the chagrin of Darth Vader and Palpatine; inspired the shock and awe from George W. in defense of, and one-upmanship over Papa Bush; and tortured father-son relationships have produced authoritarian tragedies from Shakespeare's Henry IV to Adolf to Saddam to Donald.

And I have spent many sleepless nights worrying about the sins of fathers being visited upon their sons, with my own equally sublime and vexing crucible of three teenage sons forging their own liberation from occupying forces.

My father was career-military and well versed in the fascination with war, from the day he dropped out of high school to enlist to thirty years later when the National Guard kicked him out for his expanding waistline. His pride and identity in the military were on full view, with Old Glory flying in the front yard between the kitschy gnomes and wishing well in the small, manicured front yard, the "Field Artillerymen Do It with A Bang!" bumper sticker, miniature combat boots that hung, always polished, from the rearview mirror, and the same high and tight buzz cut that he wore until the day he died.

He and I were in a perpetual state of fighting various battles within a lifelong and archetypal narrative of war. At times he sought out the battles to proclaim his authority and alpha-ness, but as I grew into broader shoulders and expanded opinions, it was I who sought out confrontation.

Some of the battles were just, even noble, understanding the conquest as God's will for his chosen warriors. Beaches were stormed, with good guys in olive green, while the bad guys were hidden behind brown shirts and iron crosses and sundry blitzkriegs. Some of the battles were fought guerilla-style, with shadowy enemies skulking in jungles set ablaze in cancerous hues of red, yellow, and orange, veiled in a haze of alcohol and opium and unwitting massacres. Some were icy and cold, with countries and continents separated behind walls of iron and stubborn grudges and secrets whispered by spies in dark corners.

But the most intense and even bloody were the wars fought over an imagination—an idea, a resistance movement, the anticipated fate of a young boy who longed for something different—that resisted being occupied or colonized. It was a hill upon which I was willing to die. Or even kill to defend it.

There were moments of détente for sure, times when mutually assured destruction was avoided or at least delayed while we hunkered down in opposing missile bays, fingers still precariously hovering over buttons. Or a tenuous peace was negotiated through my mother's odd and forceful will. There were even a few ticker-tape parades, killing of fatted calves during prodigal returns, and sharing swigs of bourbon after having vanquished a common enemy.

But the terms of surrender and armistice were always abundantly unclear. Until this particular moment, as I held the metal box of his ashes in my cold hands.

I looked skyward into the yaw of a cold Pittsburgh November. The battleship gray clouds held the mournful secrets of yet unfallen snow. The cold pierced the thin layer of gloves that held the box of my father's ashes with a stinging pain. The shovel lay against the bark of a leafless buckeye tree, the blade stained orange-brown with the first attempts at breaking the stubborn, hardened clay just over the hill behind my childhood home. The same home that the family had occupied since I was 2 years old. The same home where my restless father would be laid to rest.

My mother waited in the house just a few feet above the site that I had picked out, the grief still too raw to permit her to attend this burial rite.

There would be no funeral, no cemetery, no gathering of neighbors huddled in wool coats and scarves and Steeler beanies, their exhaled breath white against the gray sky.

No, my old man's dying wish was to have his ashes buried with the interred remains of all the family dogs over the years—a toy poodle named Romeo, a few mutts who didn't stick around long enough after having peed on the living room drapes, and a steady string of Yorkshire terriers from Frisky to Toby whose bathroom habits and eating schedules seemed to increasingly consume my father's attention until the day he died.

My father had wanted to be cremated mostly to avoid the cost and spectacle of a big funeral. He was a simple man, if not cheap, "Those goddamn funeral homes are a rip off, if you ask me. Just bury me with the dogs," he barked to no one in particular.

I think he may have also harbored an unspoken fear that no one would show up to the funeral, as like most men of his generation, he had grown increasingly isolated and friendless. He was a Catholic but hadn't been to church in years. I caught him huddled over his work bench in the basement muttering "Hail Mary's" and "Our Fathers" as he moved the beads of the Rosary between his nicotine-stained fingers. He was a stern man prone to fits of rage, but I would find him in the dark of his basement cave, with tears in his eyes, and the rote words of these ancient prayers on his lips.

The old man had also expressed that he never wanted to be confined to a pine box in the cold ground. Yet he had spent the greater part of his life in the same small box of a house for those forty years, perched on the mighty incline of Clay Drive, among the other utilitarian boxes in the neighborhood, one of three design styles that the developers imagined being filled by indiscriminate working-class families. He drove a boxy, metallic two-toned black and gold Chevette, Steelers colors he maintained, to go to work in a larger, corrugated metal box where he fabricated plastic parts and widgets for the Mine Safety Company for thirty years, watching them careen down the conveyer belt to be placed and packaged in a cardboard box and shipped out with the other boxes. He died in an orange-bricked box building at the skilled nursing facility, all sharp angles and utilitarian architecture, too sick for my mother to care for him at home in his red-bricked box of a house.

The funeral home picked his body up in a shiny, long black box of a car, transporting him in a heavy duty, black sheen bag to the back room of the boxy building on Universal Road, the plastic flowers and fake Greek columns in front serving as veneer of color and dignity for this place of such hopeful and resolute rituals for the dead. His body was transferred into the narrow, heat-retardant box of a furnace, the temperature soaring to a threshold so high as to render his body into a cragged pile of white and gray ash. Those ashes were delicately placed into the small, silver-metal box that I held in my hands. They transmitted the cold of this grey November day, heavy with the anticipation of winter. It coursed from the metal to my fingers, transmitting the cold throughout my entire body, and into my soul.

A single distant jet crossed the sky above, its white exhaust muddled with the foreboding puff of clouds. I noticed its tiny distant form just seconds before the sound waves of the muffled roar of its engines, like a Willie Nelson ditty, his gravelly lyrics just a beat or two behind the melody. The memories of my father, those true and those imagined in a haze of sorrow and longing, have always seemed to be just a beat or two behind the actual arc of his life. And I have lived a lifetime tending to that gap between sight and sound, between the real and the imagined. I have tended that gap, caressed it, given it refuge, recoiled from it, remembered it, forgotten it, ignored it, buried it, and unearthed it.

The memories are sporadic and hazy, it seems but I choose to reify the violent times, the fits of rage breaking through the quiet desperation of a man unfulfilled. Swiss film director Daniel Schmid has said that "Memory is the historical accumulation of lies." Which of my memories are lies, mere creative manipulations of a murky recollected event, constructed to make me appear more heroic in their retelling, and which of them are actually rooted in true events? I have exaggerated the primitive ways and means of my father and all of my family; it couldn't have been as bad as I imagined…could it?

I tell the stories, nonetheless, hoping that by repeating them I may experience a degree of accommodation to their malignancy, and they might lose their sting. My family harbors secrets and lies and varying layers of untruths, adopting their own stubborn strategy of keeping the pain and the stigma of violence at bay. I am the one left to tell the stories, like Ishmael cleaving to a misbegotten coffin, fostering my own truths, nobly resolute in my efforts toward reconciliation, or in less gracious moments, vengeance. Out of a perverse reverence for those secrets and their potential for further destruction, we dare not unwind the complicated past. We do not speak to one another. The silence renders those memories and recollections to a state of maddening unknowing.

I wonder aloud if the breadth of these stories can be true. I have merely participated in an accumulation of lies, a texturing of the canvas of memory, pushing the paints around with the brush of narrative to make order and beauty from the madness. If no one else dares to remember them or resists my retelling, where does truth differentiate from mere exaggeration or bald lie? My family's silence denies access to a confirming source, so I am left batting these memories around, like a kitten pawing at a skein of wool, hoping for unwinding.

The mind is powerfully complicit in this exercise, selectively parsing out the memories and reifying those that allow for imagining a more functional future. As renowned trauma expert Peter Levine has described, "…we aspire to create a future more adaptive, rewarding and beneficial than our past." I have created a narrative loop about my father and his violent tendencies, and the stories serve me well. I can pull out any number of examples to share with my empathic brethren—the story a well-polished gem that I keep hidden away in a special pouch in an unseen, deep coat pocket until I need to pull it out in dramatic flourish.

"I am not like him, can't you see?" I implore interested and uninterested onlookers alike, spinning the gem in the palm of my hand to reveal its multiple facets. In fact, not only am I not like him, but I have surpassed him in every way as a father, husband, and man. I am not my father. I have the stories to prove it.

But I am my father's son. And I am the father of my three sons. I exist in this delightful and vexing in-between. I persist sublimely preserved, at times de-animated in a liminal state, like an exotic scarab captured in deep hues of amber. Or similar to my father, I remain pickled in those same deep amber hues of Jack Daniels bottles hidden away in the pantry.

Regardless of how I choose to remember him though, his influence and the influence of his father and all of their fathers persist in a generational cascade. Those influences inhabit my DNA, as science is beginning to discover and affirm the version of the jealous God of Israel in Hebrew holy writ, who promises to visit the iniquity of the fathers on their children and their children's children.

Could I dare to remember him differently? And in that transmuted remembering, could I reconcile my past, and his past, and the beautiful tension of past and future for my boys?

It would begin, I assured myself, in a moment of sufficiently attentive grief, in how I tended to this metallic box of his ashes, of dust and crags and textured surface area of memory. It has always been a profound responsibility to tend to the burial of one's parents, practiced by the Jews in the early Roman Empire and described in Christian holy writ, when one of Jesus's roadies asks permission to leave the Tour to tend to the burial of his father.

"Let the dead bury the dead," Jesus retorts, one of the most deconstructed and dangerously misappropriated lines of the Christian gospel. There were even two burials, the first a standard one, and the second, called an *ossilegium*, when the bones from the decomposed corpse were collected, cleaned, and placed into an ossuary limestone box for safe and reverent keeping, often in the family tomb. Only then was the person deemed truly dead and his soul able to reunite with the ancestors. It is theorized that this second burial was the event that Jesus's tour roadie was asking permission to attend.

The utilitarian and unadorned metal box of my father's ashes lay in my cold, reddened fingers—no more than a few pounds, yet its gravity weighed heavily on me, my boys, on their lives, on the lives that came before them, and the lives that were yet to be. The dead burying the dead.

If I could tend to my father's remains with sufficient reverence, then perhaps my father's soul could attain the peace and equanimity that evaded him during his 72 years spent on this small swath of land behind the enclave of single-family homes on the enormously steep Clay Drive. Followers of this second burial practice believed that such reverence would inspire the dead to look favorably on the living and put in a good word with the gods or God of their choice, paying back the dutiful son with blessings and good deeds. Perhaps a karmic pay-it-forward mechanism to ensure that my boys would one day do me the same favor.

"Eh…worth a shot," I sighed to no one in particular, as the strained white breath from labored digging filtered into the frigid air.

The thought was interrupted, swirling back from mournful, perseverating thoughts to the cold immediacy of that bitter winter day. A snap from a dried twig alerted me that I was not alone. Turning slowly, I fully expected to see my father's bedraggled spirit, clad in chains and army boots from a militarized adaptation of ghosts of Christmas past, a bit early on this mid-November day. Or he would appear in the garish black and gold vintage Pirates gear of the 70's, singing the teams' inspired disco anthem, "We are Family," with a James Earl Jones voice-over from Field of Dreams fame, skulking over to ask to have a catch.

Instead, I was drawn face to face, captivated in a mutual wide, brown-eyed stupor, with a small gathering of white-tailed deer just yards away. Deer were a common sight in what passed for a small forest behind the houses in the old neighborhood, competing habitat for the animals and the expanding ring of working-class suburbs christened with the fervor of the blue-skied dreams of the late 1950's. Those woods hosted various wars and other skirmishes between the testosterone-laced set of my childhood friends, the backdrop for G.I. Joe reconnaissance missions and duels between our favorite superhero characters. I still maintain that Hulk could break out of Spiderman's web.

Hunting has always been a regular part of my family life. We lived in the heart of gun country; the halls of the high school were always a bit emptier on the first day of buck season, and my old man's rifles hung conspicuously in the gun rack adorning the cracking light blue paint of the basement cinder block wall. There was a small pistol in the headboard of my parent's bed, nestled inches from my father's head each slumbering night. I was raised on multiple viewings of the *Deer Hunter* in lieu of Sesame Street, delighting and fearing those disturbing Russian roulette scenes multiple times by the time I was eligible to apply for my first hunting license. My old man hoped that it would toughen me up.

My father would disappear for long weekends during my youth with my neighbor, Andy, and the other neighborhood dads. Andy, a long-haul trucker with an expansive gut that poured out over his grease-stained jeans and the mottled and ruddy red nose of standard-issue neighborhood alcoholic, had inherited a hunting camp in the hills of Somerset, a sleepy wooded enclave just east of Pittsburgh in the celebrated God's country of the Allegheny Mountains.

As a young boy my robust imagination conjured up images of camouflaged warriors, painted faces like John Rambo or Terminator-era Schwarzenegger, slogging through the woods on the prowl for their elusive kill. I was proud of my father, imagining him providing for his family and along the way, honoring the spirit of the deer by ferociously biting a deep mouthful of the freshly vanquished beast's heart like I had seen in romantic and fetishized Native American portrayals on the big screen.

They never seemed to return with fresh kill besides the carcasses of Iron City beer cans and pelts of McDonald's Big Mac wrappers. There was one exception, though, when the triumphant hunting party returned, whooping, and hollering, with the remains of a noble, antlered beast ignobly adorning the front of a forest green station wagon with knotted rope from my mother's clothes drying line. I peered inquisitively into the deer's eyes, vacant and staring, which failed to see its camouflaged predators in time, my own eyes tearing up with confusion and loss, hoping that my father wouldn't see me. He pushed me away from the car before his buddies took note of my softness.

There was a regaling of stories into the night, as my father and his buddies became increasingly drunk, their heroics more exaggerated with each gulp. Scenes like this had been repeated around fires for thousands of years; my father and his buddies performed this ancient ritual in the glow of the living room television. I remember trying to figure out who this man was, my father, how animated he was with his friends, in contrast to how de-animated he was around my mother and me most times. He hadn't pulled the trigger, but he looked and sounded virile and potent to my young eyes, capable of living life, giving life, even taking life.

I stubbornly persisted at the kitchen table over the next few weeks, eating the peculiar and exotically gamey venison stew, venison steak on the grill, venison jerky, and all the other ways my mother creatively prepared meals from his share of the hunting spoils. My hunting career was over before it began, perhaps because my overly dramatic and emotional response to the sprawled and lifeless body of the deer could not be trusted in the wild. My sensibilities were foreign to my father and judged as a liability. Something had changed between my father and me after that. He continued at various attempts to "toughen me up" and threatened to "really give me something to cry about," but mostly he just ignored me, anxious and unsure of how to relate.

As the thoughts hung in the thick air of melancholy, the gathering of deer and I remained still in each other's presence, captured in a reflexive, anticipatory freeze, replaying the evolutionary drama repeated throughout the ages by hunter and hunted. I wasn't entirely sure which one I was. I had no interest in them as prey, neither meat nor trophy. I imagined that they might be after me, inviting me to unfold a mystery in what had now become holy ground in this makeshift sanctuary in the woods.

I placed the box of ashes in a cloth in my coat pocket, dutifully compelled to follow the deer, but at a distance so as not to startle them into a full run. They made their way carefully through the thicket of dried leaves and broken branches, the shrapnel of memory from the perennial vibrant glory of a Pennsylvania fall. Unlike me, the deer seemed assured of where they were going. And I followed.

Chapter Two

Don't trust children with edge tools. Don't trust man, great God, with more power than he has until he has learned to use that little better. What a hell we should make of the world if we could do what we would!

Ralph Waldo Emerson

Power, as the sages have said eloquently throughout time, is a motherfucker.

It corrupts. Absolute power corrupts absolutely. And still, it is seductive and exciting.

We begin our lives titillated by our parents' power, these grand gods and goddesses towering over us, spewing directives, and judgments from their perches aloft on Olympus or behind the curtain in the Holy of Holies. And we long for their approval, daring to approach their altars with the first fruits of our earnest childhood imaginations.

Fathers, especially, can captivate their sons at a tender age, their booming voices stirring from overwhelming silence. They tinker with things and then, magically, those things are fixed. They disappear for eight or ten hours throughout the day, returning triumphant from whatever battles we imagine them waging throughout the day. Bloodied but unbowed from the struggle. And sometimes bowed.

And their power can frighten us. From fathers of a certain age and a certain generation often comes icy silence and red-hot anger. We know that these powerful beasts can roar and writhe and stop us dead in our tracks, hopeful for the evolutionary "freeze" mechanism to distract them from their search for prey. Fight or flight tends to fail, knowing because we've tried it. It never ends well.

They vanquish us easily or catch us from behind with one fell swoop of their massive and powerful grip. Those hands. Those enormous hands that can caress, and sometimes, crush.

And sometimes they laugh. Oh, to experience the glorious, if not infrequent, pealing laughter, starting deeply in jiggling beer bellies, and rising to the deep-throated joy. Ideal fathering—rough and tumble with just enough sweetness. To suffer the sublime torture of tickle fests, of fierce but loving wrestling matches on the ground, all of us sons eager to prove our mettle and the evolving power of spindly and sinewy muscles. We long for the distant memory when fathers move past their own awkwardness with touch and lay a soft palm on our backs, three strong pats to offer affirmation without crossing the threshold to "soft" or "gay."

But vigilant, always vigilant, anticipating the backhand across the mouth instead.

We possess the remarkable power and precariousness of our imaginations—longing for that laughter and ease. Still, we take what we can. Real. Imagined. We risk the backhand to receive the pat on the back.

We learn to strategize, to be quiet during the lean times—on Sunday nights after a bad Steelers loss and the looming Monday workday breaking through the haze of beers and Jack Daniels. We grow sophisticated enough to count out the two weeks between pay days. When things aren't so tense. When mothers aren't counting out change on the kitchen table to buy groceries for the next two or three days before that magical Friday.

Pay Day. When our fathers are free. Or at least a bit freer. With their love and with their purse strings. Moms get kisses. Dads get a cold case of beer. Then dads get happy. For a bit at least. Then they get angry. You never knew quite when to expect which.

Pay day Fridays meant going out for pizza at Mohan's Bar and Grill. During Lent it was fried fish sandwiches from Leo's Bar at the town bowling alley, the buns unable to hold the full glorious, golden brown, Pope-approved fish filets sticking out proudly from the bun that could not contain them.

Power, so often for men, is defined by our work. Work provides a sense of dignity, fostering self-respect and convincing the world and ourselves that we may actually matter. It is our fundamental duty to move and act in the world, the natural tendency of masculine energy to move out and up. The culture, flexing its own power, has diluted, and deluded this noble and natural intention and driven it into a shadowy, consuming corporate structure—subjugating it into an obsessive thrust towards "earning a living." And the collective corporate framework has further reified this movement by maximizing shareholder profits as law—individual souls be damned. Most of us are simply cogs in that machine, highly replaceable and mostly irrelevant.

My father was one of those mostly irrelevant and irreplaceable cogs. He even worked a job that literally made cogs, fabricating them at his machinist's station and watching them travel methodically down the conveyor belt to be trimmed, boxed, and shipped out to the next station of this inevitable enterprise.

Powerless. Eight-hour shifts with two 15-minute smoke and Coke breaks with a half-hour lunch to disrupt the monotony, if only for a brief moment. Gobbling down Pittsburgh-famous culinary delight of chipped ham and cheese sandwiches on white bread. Bitching about supervisors and the short-sleeved engineers who occupied the air-conditioned offices from their perch above the factory floor, Pittsburgh's version of the British upstairs-downstairs caste system.

But it wasn't always this way.

He had dropped out of Westinghouse High School and joined the Army at 17 with his mother's permission, mostly to escape from the violence of his alcoholic father. I'm sure his father thought it might make a "man" out of the "mama's boy." During this fortunate period between Korea and Vietnam, my father enjoyed the relative safety and halcyon days of the Cold War at his base in Baumholder, Germany, learning the ways of war and artillery and other sundry missile machinations. Another cog in a different machine, the war machine. But it gave him purpose and a larger meaning that we stumble towards as young men, teetering on adulthood.

I have re-discovered pictures of him, traversing the sights, sounds, and mostly the pubs of Berlin, Paris, and Amsterdam, smiling and slack-jawed with his buddies, with fashionable leather jackets and pegged blue jeans that made the European girls swoon. He got laid at least once, with the surprising Thanksgiving revelation years later when he casually confessed that he had gotten a Dutch woman pregnant when he was all of nineteen years old. He wanted to marry her and take her to the States, but she refused to leave home.

I revel in those photos, in the hopefulness and expression of life, a far contrast from the man I knew, bound by inertia, and parked in front of whatever television happened to be on in our home, mindlessly swilling from Iron City beer cans and seeking relief and comfort from lighting up one Winchester little cigar after another. Trapped under the haze of yellow smoke and cloak of futility.

He was Army-proud, reveling in the power of the artillery guns that he learned to fire in times of imagined conflict with an imagined Soviet force hellbent on America's destruction. His service afforded him a lifetime supply of hearing aids to assuage the damage from years of big bangs. And ample opportunities to embarrass his 16-yr old son driving the Chevy Chevette with the "Field Artillery Men Do It with a Bang" bumper sticker.

The Cold War was good business for weapons makers and the flowing tides of business seemed to raise a few scraggly, leaky boats like my father's. His artillery unit was the inheritor of new weapons systems as the Cold War escalated and the nuclear arms race ramped up. He became a nuclear missile tech with the Ajax and Hercules missile sites positioned strategically around the industrial epicenter that Pittsburgh once represented.

It wasn't a bad gig for a high school dropout with an Army-issued GED. He was skilled labor, that once-magic designation for the lower middle class and "working poor," able to feed a family and pay for a tract home mortgage on humble but perfectly functional three-bedroom, one bath homes perched on hills in working class suburbs. A once-decent school system, neighbors that looked and thought like you, close proximity to the Monroeville Mall, other kids for your kids to play with in this mostly Catholic neighborhood, the hierarchy of multiple siblings resulting from the dangerous alchemy of too many beers, horniness, and natural family planning.

His identity was wrapped up in this job. It afforded him immense pride. It offered a dose of dignity that had evaded him throughout his mostly hard life. He walked tall and had a purpose that was bigger than himself, even if it was in service of mutually assured nuclear destruction for the planet. It even gave him a new name, "Herk," after the sleek and powerful missiles nestled in the silos of the metro Pittsburgh hills and vales. He bore the name of his father, John David Herzog, which I imagine evoked discomfort in him, as the man was not exactly worthy of role model or elder status. John David Herzog, Jr. somehow scored the birthright even though he was the second son. His mother, Phyllis, whom he adored called him "Jack." Everyone else knew him as "Herk."

Back in its days of the steel mill boom, Pittsburgh was deemed a valuable industrial target by the Russians according to the US government and its partner in war crimes, the burgeoning military-industrial powers. Pittsburgh was surrounded by a "ring of steel," the pride inducing name for the various nuclear missile sites that blanketed the city and provided a degree of comfort for citizens digging backyard bunkers and school children cowering under desks during nuclear attack drills. Those silos and the missiles they harbored just a button push away from nuclear winter lined the pockets of executives at the companies that produced them, brought jobs and an expanding tax base to the Pittsburgh suburbs, and even raised the earning power of a high school dropout from the artillery unit at the National Guard base.

My father struggled with school and reading was not always particularly easy, even with his self-selected reading material of John Wayne biographies, Military Modeler magazines, or Louis L'Amour novels. Or the stack of Playboys in the garage, insisting that he read them for the articles when I discovered them magically and gratefully in my adolescence. Still, he persevered at this job and the training modules he was required to complete. He sweated and struggled and persisted through the correspondence course manuals that the job required, reading them through the night at the tiny table in the kitchen, the ashtray piled up with the stray butts from his regular evening study hours. I knew to tip toe through the kitchen if I wanted a post-dinner bowl of Frosted Flakes, hearing him scream his "goddamnits!" and "geezus-christs!" out of frustration with the challenge of the post tests that had to be completed and mailed in. Better to forego the late-night snacks altogether so as not to serve as the convenient object of his ire.

He would fly to Florida for training, back when airline travel was still a novelty for lower middle-class families like ours. My mother would proudly back his ratty suitcase for the trip and kiss him on the cheek and gently pat him on the ass when she dropped him at the airport like she was sending him to battle. I would get the obligatory t-shirt from whatever kitschy Florida tourist trap. I'm not even sure where in Florida he traveled to—it might well have been the jungles of the Amazon to my boyhood sensibilities. Upon his return I would get that T-shirt and $10 for pizza and sleep over at my buddy Phil's house. Which was heaven, until I got old enough to figure out why they wanted the house all to themselves. To the victor go the spoils.

He rarely told stories, but I was enthralled by the ones he did tell, dropped into that magical state of two-beer buzz with just the right degree of looseness…before the six-beer haze and anger. He relayed the thrill and terror of being in the missile bays during the tenuous times of the Bay of Pigs invasion—when the country was on high alert awaiting a retaliatory nuclear strike. He waxed poetic about working 12-hour shifts and sleeping for a few hours on government issue cots and itchy wool blankets, sneaking Coke and smoke breaks with his buddies and "fucking up the Commies." My dad was protecting America.

He was bigger than life, and despite the tirades and the violence, he was my hero. As it's supposed to be with fathers and sons. Until it isn't.

Good for the world, but not so good for my father and our family when Nixon signed the SALT (Strategic Arms Limitation Talks) treaties in 1972. The missiles went away as the anti-ballistic missile sites were negotiated down. The nuclear threat was deterred. The silos were cemented and sealed hermetically like tombs, the land repurposed as community parks, a Native American Cultural Center, and for my father, a bitter memory of his dream of pride and financial stability deferred.

Uttering the name Nixon in our house was the unpardonable sin, met with profanity-laced tirades. My father had a dog in that fight, and Tricky Dick kicked that dog and my father in the balls. It was just one more thing that seemed remarkably out of his control. These decisions that are the "right" thing to do, like avoiding nuclear catastrophe and WWIII, have remarkable ripple effects. Coal mines closed, fighter jet contracts canceled, pork projects shelved—they are not without their consequences, intended and unintended.

For my father, it continued his sense of diminished power, that he and subsequently his role of provider for the family were beholden to the whims of circumstance, fate, and even Richard Nixon. My father, and other fathers, may have lacked the vocabulary, but he was helpless in the understanding of his own mortality, whether he admitted it or not. When faced with the prospect of death, consciously or unconsciously, troops get mustered, wagons get circled, and evolutionary strategies kick in.

Or sometimes men simply exist in an unknowing and perpetual despair and frustration. Like my father. And our fathers.

These are not feelings that are easily processed. Grief and shame are efficiently evoked. Our fathers' generation, raised on the American ethos of silent suffering of their war heroes and cowboys, have attempted to keep those feelings at bay, stuffed and tamped down. But they leak—they have to because the human soul can only bear so much Reality, so much suffering.

Fueled by this dangerous alchemy of grief, shame, and despair, the prevailing expression for men of a certain age—and most men raised with shadowy masculinity—is anger and even rage. They, we, fight wars over it—local wars, global wars, wars within our families.

In her extraordinary book, *Gravity and Grace*, philosopher Simone Weil stated that true gods turn suffering into violence. The false gods, bent on domination, project that violence toward their partners and children, as evidenced by escalating numbers of reported domestic violence cases can attest. Their sons especially, as cycles of violence and abuse are visited on sons from their fathers, who were often subject to the same violence from their fathers. I have visited this same violence on my own sons, perhaps not as overt as my own father, but violent, nonetheless.

And the world spins round. Often on this tilted axis.

One of those glorious wrestling matches went awry with my oldest son. He had grown stronger and fiercer through puberty as his voice grew deeper, hair sprouted, and his muscles grew more sinewy and powerful. I had always given cursory effort during these matches, eventually conceding with great drama under the dogpile of my three sons. This time was different.

I had to struggle to maintain my edge, hellbent on not allowing him to flip me on my back and embarrass me in front of my tribe, my alpha status in the pack at peril. I had him on his back with my legs pressing his arms to the ground. We were both operating at a deeper evolutionary level, the elder alpha and the young upstart positioning himself for succession.

He wrenched his right arm free. and with particular velocity reached up his hand toward my face, his nails dragging across my cheek leaving a bloody scratch for all the pack to see. I was embarrassed for my ebbing power; he was embarrassed for his flowing power. We rose from the ground and shook hands in an awkward silence and went about the rest of the day. Still, I could notice him peering at me with a sheepish but proud smirk, as the scratch scabbed over and healed over the next week. He had gotten me.

Every man I speak with has a similar story, a distinct memory of an exchange, an event when power was challenged, tables were turned, and power dynamics were flipped. The boy becomes a man, surpassing his father's power—even for just a moment. Or the man knows when it could have happened and when it should have happened.

I had returned home for my customary obligatory holiday visit, too big for my goddamn britches, as my father might have described. I had been through enough therapy in my early twenties to begin naming the family dysfunction but not enough to keep my anger from bubbling over. I'm still working on that last part.

My mother, father, and I were all gathered in our tiny kitchen. My father parked in front of the TV and my mother futzed in the kitchen. I uttered something typically sarcastic to my mother in response to one of her directives as a means of sublimated anger, a skill that I had unfortunately honed over years of repressed anger.

"Watch your mouth, smart ass!" my father threatened, leering at me with that sidewards glance that used to strike fear in my heart.

"Sit down, old man, I could kick your ass all over this kitchen."

I'm not sure where it came from. There was certainly no forethought or reason for constructing such a silly sentence. But it came from such a deep place. A place of grief. A place of shame. And certainly, from a place of anger.

"You two just stop it," my mother exhorted, shifting awkwardly back to her pot on the stove.

The tension hung awkwardly in the air, my father and I unable to move towards reconciling or even making eye contact. I had to get out, to be anywhere but in that kitchen, in that house, in that family. I was scared of my own power, and my father was scared of it, too. Or at least afraid that his own power was ceding; the last vestige of the power that he had over his son was gone now, too. It was a moment of quiet despair for him, an exhilarating one for me.

I grabbed my sneakers and ran out of the house, grateful for an escape. I ran until I could run no further. Then I walked and kept walking with no sense of where I was going. The neighborhood offered mammoth hills to work out my manic energy, legs pumping and chest heaving, my breath chugging white in the December cold. I ended up at my old high school, just miles from my childhood home, unsure even of how I had arrived there. My knees ached, my lungs burned, and I began sobbing tears that had been pent up for years.

I eventually made my way back home. My father and I made no mention of our exchange. We returned to our respective corners, both a bit bloodied after this last round waiting for the judges' scorecards to be announced. Winner by unanimous decision, spoken or unspoken. Something had changed. I walked a little taller and more confident. My father slumped a bit more, it seemed, at his usual place at the kitchen table. I ached for him while also understanding that this shift in power had been long overdue.

The exchange between father and son, this shift in power, need not always be so dramatic or steeped in the violence of father-son encounters. A client I have worked with in my therapy practice, an older gentleman whose father had been long deceased, related to me an exchange that he had with his father when he was 13 years old. My client, in his mind, was on the cusp of adulthood and despite the warm relationship with his father, had decided that it was no longer acceptable to kiss his father on the lips when he went to bed. He told me how it broke his father's heart, but that his father understood. Heart breaking but necessary.

The indelible memory had been on his mind since it was the anniversary of his father's death. This particular day, this particular session, this particular memory—he still wrestled with it. He tenderly offered to show me the program from his father's funeral, with the family photo of him, his parents, his six siblings surrounding them, his father beaming with pride at the center of the photo of his large, Catholic brood. A bit of a hoarder, my client performed this informal ritual wearing the same fleece sweatshirt that his father had been wearing in that family photo. In that program from the funeral. On that day.

Heart breaking but necessary, these rites of passage.

How then do we participate in this transformation with integrity, and also with the sacrifice of heartache that the gods demand. Heartache may be what transforms us, for if we do not engage the shadow, the hard emotions, the shadowy ancestral histories, then we may remain unchanged. We may become even more frustrated since we have edged toward the precipice of true change—personally, culturally, and ancestrally—without actually changing. Authentic power is born from risking transformation. It is difficult if not impossible to discover new lands without letting go of the shore.

We can find exemplars of men who have dared to transform and operate from this sense of authentic power, men who have resisted the seduction of conventional and cursory models of power that the world offers. These are our true Elders. The men we wish to emulate as we transition into Elderhood ourselves. Daring transformation impels us to become worthy of this title as Elder, willing to participate in the world, to act with intention born from wisdom as true masculine power and energy aspires while acting with compassion, humility, and fierceness.

Our anger can transform into fierceness. Shame into humility and conscience. Grief into compassion.

This story is not a new one, having been told and retold in different forms through time. The *Iliad*, an ancient tale of war, journey, and return, regales the story of the mighty Trojan warrior Hector. Hector is noble in his mission, in his sacrifice for the people of Troy, responding to his wife Andromache's pleas for him to retreat from the front lines to stay with her and their infant son Astyanax, "…I would have too much shame before the men and women of Troy if I were not in battle." Even while reifying his being compelled to remain in battle, he longs to be in relationship with his young son.

Hector reaches for his son, but the boy recoils in fear because Hector has forgotten to remove his bloody and dusty armor, stained, and soiled by the battle. He remains in liminal space, a space of transformation between the battlefield and the presence of his family. Hector could have easily dropped into a feeling of shame for the effect he had on his young son. He could have easily projected that shame onto the boy for his "weakness" or onto his wife for her "failures" to mind the boy's courage.

Instead, Hector, realizing his own foibles as a man, warrior, and father but not taking them too seriously, throws his head back in laughter. It is a liberating act. He is free to be responsive in the moment, not reactive in anger or shame. He and his wife exchange a smile as he removes the armor that stands between and separates him and his son. Still fierce and intending fully to return to battle, Hector operates from a transformed place of humility and compassion to move from his position of power to kneel before his son in a loving embrace.

He lifts the child up to the heavens, to his gods, "Zeus, make this child of mine strong. And one day, on seeing him return from battle, may one of you say, 'He is far stronger than his father.'"

The power dynamics of the past and even the present cede to the power of hope, the power of the future. Hector needs not be threatened by the prospect of his son's power, needs not be violent or shaming or avoidant of the transition of power between father and son. It can even be ritualized and celebrated, the humility of the father actually informing and infusing both father and son with even more power—power that can be fierce and tender.

The battles resume. Hector returns to the frontlines. He is remembered as the greatest Trojan warrior, even in the grisly way in which the angry and vengeful Achilles kills him. Astyanax is killed as an infant. The Greeks feared that if the boy were allowed to live, he would seek revenge and rebuild Troy. They feared the repetition and recapitulation of old models of masculine power; they feared that the boy would grow powerful enough to wrest the power from them.

The recycling of this kind of masculine power and the battles they provoke are harrowing and bear great trauma and suffering. The battles, the lust for power, longs to be transformed. We participate in transformation by remembering father and son differently, naming the grief and the possibility of its power to rend us open and change us. We participate in transformation when the boy inspires the father to remove his armor, to reveal and expose his heart that the armor was meant to protect. The father dares to hope for the future, for the assumption of even greater power for his boy, of authentic power containing both fierceness and tenderness alike.

I dare to remember my own father. I dare to forgive him for his sins of commission and omission. I dare to imagine a different future for my sons. I dare to surrender my hope for a different past.

I have wrestled with blame and grief, especially after he died without any seeming resolution to our relationship, but no longer. I understand him as I stumble into middle age. I can even empathize with him, knowing that my own professional pursuits and dreams have been deferred by the demands of family life and "earning a living." I won't author the Great American Novel, play catcher for my beloved hometown Pirates, or rock with Led Zeppelin.

Sometimes I even throw my head back in reasoned and reconciled laughter. Sometimes I am freed. Freed to forgive. Freed to love.

As I move further into the obligatory householder role with my own three boys and the sacrifices, both sacred and profane, that their needs and their lives demand, I understand my father's sacrifices. Some were deliberate and others thrust upon him by circumstance, but he tried to be different, to do fathering slightly differently than his own father. I long to be able to tell him all this, all of my gratitude, in contrast to the ungracious things that I said when he was alive, when I was angry and grieving.

I long to do better, to love deeper, and to father differently. But I know I can only participate in this kind of healing and the fruit it may bear by engaging in forgiveness.

This book is in many ways a love letter to him, a plea for forgiveness for the things I said and didn't say. It is an ode to let him know that I've forgiven him for the harsh things that he said and more so, for the imperfectly perfect ways in which he tried to father and even love.

I want to tell him that I'm proud of him for fathering one degree differently than he was fathered, and I hope that he is gratified and proud that I am parenting my boys with expanded and compassionate degrees of difference. I long to understand that his rage and anger were simply expressions of his own unprocessed grief and shame. To understand that the culture around him also contributed to his alienation and loneliness. To understand that he suffered at the hands and fists of his own father, and without resource or eldering, was projecting all of that onto his only begotten son.

And his pain. I want to understand the pain from his experience of his father's traumas—the generational wounding that became part of our family culture. The same wounding that is part of our family cultures. I want to imagine that this process is part of my father's healing and for the healing of our ancestors—of all the fathers who've struggled with their unmetabolized grief, shame, and anger, that dangerous and provocative and at times unholy triad of emotions that the culture has resisted in allowing men to experience and process.

I long to comprehend that it all occurred as it needed to. And still, that fathering can and must be transformed. For my own healing and most achingly and longingly, for the healing of my sons. And their sons. And all of our sons.

Chapter Three

*It doesn't matter who my father was;
it matters who I remember he was.*

Anne Sexton

I am a man of a certain age.

And with that designation comes a whole myriad of signs and symptoms: the hairline gravitates north while the waist line descends south; rogue hairs break from the tight formation of eyebrow, ear and nostril ranks, rivaling the hirsute stylings of my Grampa' Eddie; I make grunting, effortful harrumph noises when I get up from the ground; my knees and other creaky joints contribute to the chorus, sounding like stomped bubble wrap; and most profoundly, I wait with fear and trembling for The Call.

And The Call changes everything.

Disease, tragedy, or the otherwise capricious nature of circumstance often forces us to deal with the death of a parent before we're quite ready or at least prepared, but most of us face this remarkable scenario in the throes of mid-life. Although even in mid-life it's hard to describe oneself as ready.

Freud described the death of a parent as "…the most significant event, the most decisive loss, of a man's life." The death of his own father was certainly a seminal event for Freud and, no less formidably, for the course of

Western thought, as our dear Sigmund dealt with the loss by "discovering" and proclaiming the Oedipal complex and its father-wounding as a fundamental expression of the potentially dark depths of the human unconscious.

The death of a parent can be unmooring at the very least, if not debilitating emotionally. It would take an entirely new book, or volumes, to explore the orphaning that one experiences with the death of both parents. But that first dramatic hit, that first loss is a not so gentle reminder of the existential forces at play in the universe.

Even with the textured variety of memories that our parents and their parenting hold for us, there is a certain balance, a certain wholeness or perspective that is maintained when they're both alive and just a phone call or dysfunctional, wine-laden Thanksgiving visit away. Geologically speaking, all the continents were theorized to be one big, happy lump of landmass before tectonic shifts and pressures forced the divisions that we learn about from shiny plastic maps and globes in elementary school. When a parent dies, those fractures become thrust into our consciousness, and emotionally we fashion more arbitrary lines on the maps and in the sand, imagining even more that we are on our own and responsible for our own protection as barbarians wait at every gate, primed for attack and plunder. Or maybe that's just me.

There is a certain morbid expectation of inevitability that you learn to live with, especially as you get to observe the aging process of a parent who becomes progressively sicker. While anticipating The Call I received many "small-c" calls from my mother, alerting me to the latest malady or surgery that my dad was having to endure, with the ever-expanding rows of pill bottles in tow. Misery courted the old man like a sex-starved teenage suitor, searching for the next dry hump of release and recoil.

It began with a tragic car accident in his early thirties, when my unsuspecting father's car was slammed into by an inattentive driver who blew a stop sign and blew any chance of my pop's hope for good fortune. I recall hearing my mother shriek on the phone when she heard the news, as I lay on my grandmother's living room carpet, consumed with a young five-year old boy's gravitas of Star Wars action figure play.

The accident landed him in traction in the hospital for six weeks and landed the photo of the crash scene on the front page of the local paper—the twisted metal and carnage worthy of coverage. The yellowed newspaper article remains part of family lore, tucked away in a photo album in a dark hallway closet. The enduring fallout from the crash eventually ravaged his hip with excruciatingly painful arthritis that required replacing the old, decrepit hip with a titanium one long before it was in vogue for the boomer set.

The accident was a catalyst for a cascade of other maladies and surgical procedures, robbing him of his well-being and inspiring a fatalist view of the world, remedied methodically by a stream of Jack Daniels and Iron City beer chasers. He had a big toe joint replaced; back surgery to address the orthopedic shrapnel from an imploding hip joint; double hernia surgeries to gird his strained loins; a gall bladder removed and cast away on the surgical suite's floor, among others.

My father never stood a chance.

I made the trek along the curvy, remote lanes of the Pennsylvania Turnpike from Philadelphia, my new home, to Pittsburgh, my old one, when he underwent the gall bladder procedure. Fresh out of graduate school I was beginning the ascension phase of my own life as I began to observe the soft signs of a precipitating descent for my father. My mother convinced me to make my way once again along the well-traveled path between the urban centers of Pennsylvania, a deep groove worn in the record of my young adulthood, a fair geographical distance from my family but not quite far enough to remain free from the emotional tendrils of frail parents.

"You better come home, Bobby," she implored, a seriousness in her voice that I had not heard before. She too realized the slope upon which my father was beginning to slip.

I packed up my little red Honda Civic with a weekend bag, unconsciously convincing myself that my father would be fine, that a weekend bag would be sufficient. I had my radar detector in place, the antidote to draconian Pennsylvania speeding fines, as I enjoyed the speed and verve of the seeming immortal existence of my late adolescence. I don't know if I've ever felt more alive than when I was on a road trip, sunroof open, Springsteen affirming that I was *Born to Run* , the soundtrack of this period of life reverberated from the well-considered mix tape, and the possibilities endless careening around the mountainous curves of Pennsylvania's terrain and an unlimited horizon ahead.

I made my way across the brown-green waters of the Allegheny River over one of the ubiquitous, weathering steel-girded Pittsburgh bridges to St. Margaret's Hospital. It had once existed as a small and indistinguishable community hospital that had recently grown into a more remarkable place of care after having been gobbled up by the corporate leviathan that was the University of Pittsburgh Medical Center. It had become my mother's go-to establishment for her and my father's steadily increasing health care needs, inspiring hearty "hellos" and "How yinz doin'?" from the front desk staff as we passed through the automatic doors in the lobby.

I arrived just in time to see my father being transferred from his bed onto the awaiting gurney by two broad-shouldered orderlies in light blue scrubs. While most health care providers strive mightily to maintain a patient's dignity, there is something about being clad in paper hospital gown regalia, ass exposed to the world, lying in uncomfortable anticipation on one's back that inevitably and incredulously inspires a sense of helplessness and indignity. My father, whom I had mostly known as a pillar, and often abuser, of power and authority, was completely and utterly helpless. The image was further caricatured by seeing his lower jaw sliding down into his substantial neck girth, his false teeth plucked from the maw of his thin lips and staring at us from across the room in a small container of water, like a long-forgotten lab specimen.

As I made my way toward the gurney, I could see a gentle haze of anesthesia washing over his face as the orderlies methodically clicked shut the gurney's metallic side bars, readying him for transport to the operating room. His eyes slowly and stubbornly scanned to the side across his visual field to my mother and me as we rested our arms on the gurney's rails, my mother's eyes watering and her left-hand cleaving to his. Her white gold wedding band was conspicuous only in comparison to the absence of his band, as it rested in the top drawer of the particle board nightstand next to his bed, intermingled with the rosary beads, menthol cough drops and plastic-coated copy of the Gospel.

My eyes eventually met his, and I was surprised, if not embarrassed, by the intense intimacy contained in his gaze. Heavy narcotics may have inspired it, but there was a flash of emotion that belied his usual angry and stoic demeanor. Love? Perhaps. Panic? For certain. He reached up and across the railings, up and across the years of anger and resentment, and held me in a desperate embrace, if only for a second or two. I suppose I had regularly entertained the idea that this might be the last time that I would see him alive, given his state of perpetual ill health. In the throng of this embrace that I had imagined and longed for, through the silent and stiff state of emotional detente that we had carved out over the years, I sensed the helpless dread and liberation that this was really "it," the final time that I would look upon his animated being.

And truly for the first time in my life I felt afraid. It had always been present, this existential fear that I had mused about intellectually for years, pursuing my penchant for obscure, dour French philosophers, and listening to wonderfully melancholic Cure songs. But now it landed with the force of an anvil pressing against my chest, making it difficult for me to breathe. I placed my arm over my mother's shoulder, working gently to pull her away from the gurney.

My mother and I didn't speak about the awkward intimacy of the moment. We couldn't speak about it, for we lacked a common language to do so. When it came to matters of authentic emotion we were like a tourist and a local stumbling to find understanding, resorting to gestures and Google Translate and finally just speaking more loudly before giving up.

It wasn't the last time that I saw my father. He pulled through the surgery with decent post-op meds and a new scar to add to the expanding fold. He liked to brag about his survivalist stubbornness through pithy little sayings that I'm sure he overheard during his long military life, "Well, Bobby, God don't want me and the devil's afraid I'll take over." And we certainly didn't dare broach the subject of his unwitting foray into emotional expression. This was tacitly prohibited within our family culture, and any attempts were met with condemnation or at least mere platitudes, "No sense complainin', nobody listens to me anyway."

I felt changed a little bit, though. I was overwhelmed by an abject sense of sadness, knowing that it would not be long before his inevitable decline. I grieved more in knowing that somewhere beneath the steely and silent veneer lay an interiority of real emotion and desperation to connect, to navigate some kind of relationship with me, his only son, the sole blood heir to his ways of longing. I longed for him to express a capacity, an inkling of expression that might convince me that all of the shame and all of the abuses were merely misdirected and misguided attempts to be loving. I had spent my entire life, not to mention an abundance of will and money in therapy, to understand why he seemed to *dislike* me so much.

It seemed a profound, if not brief, moment when the anger and grief slowly melted away into a sort of pathos about my father, an evolving compassion for his limitations that could almost broach the gap between the imagined father that I longed for and the man he was.

Almost. But not quite. And my therapist knew it for sure.

The line you never want to hear from your therapist, "Why don't you think about coming two times a week." I watched in earnest from the discomfort of the therapy couch as my expressions of dread helped to pay for a new pool just beyond the window of her home office.

Several more of my pop's surgical procedures and my own wanderlust-inspired moves from Pennsylvania to New Mexico found me finally nestled in the hippy confines of San Francisco's North Bay. The father of three boys of my own, I had sublimated the passions of unending mid-life crises into pursuing a doctorate in psychology, embodying, I suppose, another of my father's lines, "If you can't beat 'em, join 'em." A professional pursuit for sure, but also an unconscious attempt made manifest in the service of tiptoeing through the morass of my family's dysfunction.

Watch what you wish for. The first book assigned in my first syllabus in my first class was The Father, written by an earnest, erudite Italian Jungian called Luigi Zola. I poured through the book in a matter of days, coursing and cursing through his interpretation of actual and archetypal fathering. As I read through the book, I conjured up competing images of the raging and powerful memories of the father of my youth with the frail, helpless father of my middle-age.

Another of the symptoms of this stage of life, as I've had affirmed by other accidental pilgrims on the journey, is finding oneself fully and self-consciously awake at 3AM, staring at the ceiling wondering anxiously about mortgages and term paper deadlines and the San Francisco Giants' need for a decent left fielder with power. One particular night I resolved at least two of those problems, content that decent starting pitching could cover up a multitude of weak lineup sins. I lulled myself happily back to sleep by five, grateful for at least another hour of slumber before my alarm beckoned me to another day's work.

And then the phone rang.

It was the land line, a sort of Bat Phone that was used mostly to be able to call from the road to speak with the boys for a few more years before tween and adolescent pressure tactics inspired cell phone purchases. The only other person who called on that number was my mother, as she refused to participate in any technological advance beyond the VCR.

Sure enough, as the predawn haze cleared a bit, I recognized the Pittsburgh area code against the green backlight of the phone's display, glowing brightly in the dark. My stomach dropped, my knees buckled a bit, and my head swirled with images of funerals, wakes, and memories of my old man waiting for me after every football practice, with Frisky, the yippy Yorkshire Terrier of my youth. The stupor was broken by loud rings in the silence of early morning. I swallowed hard and pressed the "talk" button, certain that things had already changed.

The ringing stopped abruptly. I fumbled in the dark to hit the "redial" button, losing the action of opposable thumbs in my panic. The phone methodically beeped out the 10-digit number heralding the news of my fatherless existence. A quickening pulse boomed at my temples, my jaw clenched as I waited for my mother to pick up, the phone cradled in my increasingly sweaty palm. Who would I be now as a fatherless son? I am about to become the family patriarch. What if my mother asks me to compose a eulogy? What could I say about this simple man who I wished to be more complicated, more compelling?

Images of my father from family photos flashed across my mind's eye—as a young, hopeful kid out of boot camp stationed in Germany; standing beside me at my first Communion, clad unmercifully in wide lapels; holding my baby son, Arlo, both of them sporting the same bald, wide-eyed, ample fat folded expression. My father's eyes slightly tinged with yellow, reflective of the years of drinking or the first sign of the cancer spreading from his lungs to his liver. I could even smell his strange alchemical scent of Old Spice, Winchester little cigars and Iron City beer.

Finally, I heard my mother's throat clear as the call connected after what seemed like an eternity.

"Hello, Yo?" I whispered, my voice trembling. I used the shortened version of my mother's name Yolande, having abandoned the idea of Mother long ago.

"Oh, sorry, Bobby. I must have dialed you by mistake. Listen, I'm on hold with Verizon. Can I call you back?"

"Whaaat?" I stammered. "Dad's OK?"

"Yeah, why? I gotta' go. Isn't it early there?"

Click. Dial tone. Loud beeps.

The operator's monotone voice, "If you'd like to place your call again, please hang up…"

I crawled back into bed, my heart racing, reaching over to turn the alarm off on my phone, convinced that I may not ever sleep restfully again.

Chapter Four

*I don't love men.
I love what devours them.*

André Gide

What kid wouldn't want a grandpa with a peg leg? It would be easy to conjure up technicolor visions of swashbuckling pirates losing limbs to bloodthirsty sharks while in hot pursuit of buried treasure, parrot on the shoulder, a cask of rum at the ready . I thought I was the envy of all my friends, since my grandfather waddled around on an old wooden prosthesis, long before the precision titanium models became en vogue. I don't remember much about the man except for the echo of his honey-varnished cane against the hollow of his straight-planed leg, the pant leg raised to reveal a sagging black sock against the grain of his prosthesis that inspired a young boy's memory of tales of Captain Hook.

I imagined him regaling me with wondrous tales of bravery on the battlefield, my own private Sergeant York—pelted with shrapnel in his leg while storming a machine gun turret on the beaches of Normandy or being harpooned with a Japanese bayonet while dragging a wounded buddy through the jungles of the South Pacific. Imagine my disappointment when, finally, my father shared the truth, sighing and rolling his eyes at my romantic and misplaced imagination. In a manner somewhere slightly south of romantic, he informed me that my grandfather lost his leg when the sizable metallic girth of a train wheel crushed the long bone of his leg while he lay passed out in a drunken stupor on the track.

The old man, John David Herzog, Sr., would win bar bets at the local Wilkinsburg taverns, betting the other sucker patrons that he could stick a pen knife through his trousers into his leg without wincing. There were many notches in that wooden leg.

There has never been an abundance of family lore to be shared at family gatherings, since the truth was always a little more tragic, if not stranger, than the fiction I imagined. My mother was an only child, and my father had a brother, Albert, whom he stopped talking to after my grandmother's funeral at the behest of my mother, who hated Al's wife. When I asked about the three boy cousins I'd never met, my father would reply tersely, "You ain't missin' much." So, not remarkably, it was not standing room only at our family reunions.

The family on my father's side immigrated from Germany, making their way from the expectant shores of Ellis Island to settle in the dusty coal netherworld of Tyrone, Pennsylvania, dark and cold and foreboding like a familiar German emotional expanse. My great-grandfather Albert Herzog was on the original rolls of the city census, but my genealogy pursuits have unearthed little more information about the Herzog men save for their habit of siring male offspring and bathing themselves in a gene pool filled with cheap beer and even cheaper whiskey.

My father never added much to the family narrative, stoic until the end despite my numerous inquiries into our generational epic. His descriptions of his own father, John, always began with the adjective "mean"—"mean son-of-a-bitch," "mean ol' cuss," "mean bastard." Not at all congruous with my images of swashbuckling pirates or brave war heroes. John had to go on disability after losing his leg, finding his purpose, and losing his monthly government check at the bottom of a bottle.

He was naturally quite good at being a drunk and practiced perfecting his craft. He married my grandmother, a splendid spit-fire Irish woman named Phyllis, whom my father adored. She died from complications from diabetes when I was young, so I don't have any memories of her, save for a collection of opaque stories that my mother has shared. She took my mother in, a scared divorcee with two kids from her first marriage, including my oldest half-brother, Chuck, conceived at seventeen. Phyllis taught my mother to cook basic meals that never aspired to culinary heights beyond chipped corn beef on toast or beans and wieners spiced with ketchup and cinnamon, but it was as close to love as she had ever experienced. She taught her the utilitarian skills that passed for the love of a mother in the 60's and taught my father how to pick up the pieces, both literally and figuratively after one of my grandfather's frequent drunken rages. After her death, my father rarely spoke about her, if at all, but when he did it was in hushed tones and reverence typically reserved for saints.

After having left her during those rages, John discovered that there wasn't much of a market for drunk, unemployed men with a peg leg as a prospective spouse, despite his noble efforts. So, he limped back up the stairs of the family's storefront, walk-up apartment in the working-class town of Wilkinsburg, apologized for the drinking and raging and abuses and Phyllis took him back in without question. She was a practical woman, if nothing else and limited in her options as a potentially divorced woman with one kid and a few bucks made on the side as a seamstress taking in tattered and torn clothes from the neighbors. Nine months later my father was born, another boy to join my Uncle Albert, nine years my father's senior and named for the original Herzog scion in America. Despite being the second boy, my father got the birthright, bearing the name and the generational onus of John Jr. Naming boys was a big deal in those days, long before our generation of parents became obsessed with finding cute, ironic hipster names for their male offspring.

The Herzog boys endured what I can only imagine was a series of traumas and abuses that mental health professionals today would name progressive trauma or adverse childhood experiences. Broken shards and various rudimentary tools of my father's own violent rages were the archaeological fragments unearthed during my earnest efforts at digging through the dusty layers of family silence, offering clues to the tone and dark hues of the family culture in which he was reared. Albert survived long enough to join the Navy and see the world while scraping paint off the hulls of various ships.

My father was left behind to serve as the lone target of my grandfather's shame and vitriol, internalizing a skewed and schizoid image of what it meant to be a man. He dropped out of high school to join the army at the tender age of seventeen, tricking my grandfather during a drunken stupor to extend his blessing and sign the papers to authorize his underage sojourn into the military world of spit-shined boots and crisp hospital corners on the sheets of his bunk, a welcome, albeit compulsive, oasis of order within the emotional chaos of childhood.

My father died with the same high and tight hair style that he sported fresh out of boot camp in the fifties. He adopted the persona to match his coif. Boots always polished, "Field Artillery Men Do It with a Bang" and "These Colors Don't Run" bumper stickers on his late model Japanese import, and John Wayne videos on a continuous loop in the VCR. The last day of school for me ended the same each year, picked up at the bus stop and whisked away to Eddie's Barber Shop on Saltsburg Rd. for my own crew cut, lest my own hair dare to touch the tops of my ears, inspiring neighborhood taunts of "bald-headed Bobby" to "bald-headed booby" to just "boob," the nickname that followed and cursed me through junior high.

It seems that my generation, at least in the provincial halls of the first ring of working-class suburbs outside of Pittsburgh, was blessed with the luxury, and burden, of self-discovery. I enjoyed the fruits of my father's consistent if not inglorious labor, enjoying the relative freedom that remained just out of reach of his generation, as he and his cohort could only watch from the outside at those who were smart, lucky, or manipulative enough to profit from the post-war financial windfall, the Big Sky Dream that inspired track housing and strip mall sprawl.

These guys were the "suits," as my father called them—the college-educated, short-sleeved engineers who occupied the glass walled offices high above his factory floor and even higher on the company pay scale. The ones he and his buddies derided but longed to be, or at least whose paychecks they envied, barely able to scrape together a few spare dollars every pay day to buy a case of Iron City and fried fish sandwiches for the whole family from the bowling alley tavern on Lenten Fridays.

This was a similar trap that remarkably influenced his relationship with me. He longed for me, I suppose to do better than him, to enjoy a life with afternoons spent carefree at Pop Warner football practice, to be able to pursue a college degree, to live without the more obvious traumas of an alcoholic father. And he sacrificed nobly to afford me these opportunities, drinking enough to numb himself to life but not enough to be as abusive as his own father, employing me as look-out for my mother as he sneaked sips from the bottle of Jack Daniels, he kept in the bottom drawer of the dining room curio. He even sold his collection of guns that graced the walls of our cement-blocked basement to pay for books for my first year of college.

But then I became a "suit," with a fancy college diploma and eventually an even fancier graduate school one, writ holy and large in embossed Latin script. I can only imagine the cognitive dissonance that he might have entertained, seeing me fulfill part of the destiny that he had imagined but also knowing that it could and would create irreparable separation between us.

I took advantage of the time that both my mother and father chose to parent through threats and derision to hole up in the corner of my second-floor bedroom, trembling but determined to find an escape from the downstairs world. Time passed methodically under the angled core board walls as I perused pages of lions and witches and wardrobes and heroes of my youth that graced the sports section of the Pittsburgh Press and the consciousness of a boy hoping for something else, imagining anything else.

While lost in the fantastical world of C.S. Lewis's Narnia I imagined a portal through the back of that wardrobe where the perceived existential threats of boyhood existed at least manageable under the large, protective shadow of Aslan. We weren't the family to have an armoire to house my Toughskin jeans or my dad's vast collection of flannel shirts, sweatpants, and sans-a-belt slacks but there was a small, unassuming door in the back of the lone hallway closet that led to a crawl space filled with dusty Christmas decorations and forgotten family knick-knacks. I felt breathless and not a bit less exotic the first time my trembling hands opened the door, closing my eyes and hoping for a Narnian winter on the other side to save me from the emotionally dystopian nuclear family winter on this side. The disappointment that I discovered on the other side did not prevent me from trying repeatedly, each time closing my eyes and saying a little prayer to whatever god or guardian lion or Santa Claus proxy I could conjure up to make my wish come true.

"Bobby, dinner!" my mother would exclaim, breaking the spell of hopefulness.

I would clamber down the stairs to join my parents at the small circular table in the kitchen, the hash slung, the milk poured, my parents engrossed in the night's local news that blared from the small TV in the center of the table, one of five sets that graced our little three-bedroom house. My mother would futz and dart around the kitchen, light up a cigarette and mutter to herself or bark commands at me while my father sat motionless, almost catatonic as he shoveled food into his mouth and sipped from the soon-emptied aluminum shell of that meal's second or third beer. From a young age I labored to imagine what might be going through his mind, what odd collection of thoughts tarried behind the often-inanimate face encased in loose jowls and thick neck. He would occasionally catch me staring at him and growl, "Whaaat?!" and then return to his methodical routines.

The dinner routine gave way to the evening routine, my mother splayed on the living room couch, asleep by eight as various sitcom and cop show drama blared from the TV. My father would sit motionless at the kitchen table, the inertia interrupted by draws on his Winchester little cigar or summons to the bathroom after the third or fourth beer. He would sit slumped, the shoulders meeting the wrinkled girth of his neck and head as the TV shouted louder and louder through the hazy smoke. He sat under a yellowing nicotine halo on the ceiling above the kitchen table, an indelible memory of all the nights he sat in various states of suspended animation. The nicotine stain resisted fresh coats of paint, bleeding through the attempts at covering the evidence of my dad's existence, like a stubborn cave painting persisting over generations to bear witness to the lives and machinations of the people who inhabited that particular space. "I was here," it announced. And I smoked. A lot.

I have remembered less and less of the episodes of my father's rage, giving him a pass that approximates forgiveness as the years since his death pass methodically. I remember these states of inertia more, a man's desperation captured in time and frozen there, a perpetual winter waiting for the spring thaw that never seemed to come. It was a brokenness that inspires a sort of pathos now.

Theologian and philosopher Paul Tillich wrote of the trap of such an existence that was less than human, "We do not experience unfreedom as dehumanizing because we are deprived of definite possibilities but because we are no longer able to react as whole persons. He who no longer is able to act from centeredness, from wholeness, whence all elements of his being join in an ultimate decision, has ceased to be human in the true sense of the word."

I never knew him as human, as a man, as a husband, as father. He spoke in platitudes and doled out punishment in fits of rage that regularly broke the icy silence. I begged him to tell me stories, even from an early age, not only to fill in the gaps of family lore, but as an attempt to understand him. To know that there was some "there" there. "What the hell do you want to talk about?!" he would shriek, before returning to his well-worn routines, grateful for the simplicity of the stillness punctuated by lulling History Channel narratives blaring increasingly loud from the TV as his hearing grew worse over the years of artillery blasts and factory machine humming.

I couldn't, and still can't, quite process that there was humanity within that shell of a man, an essence or persona that might break through, groaning to be known, someone to whom I could relate to or at least bump up against. I have constructed my own story about his life from the snippets of clues left from stilted conversations and stories from my brother and sister and from old black and white photographs yellowing over time in the hallway closet. There are pictures of him from his days in the Army, stationed in Germany where he looked *alive*, in a way that I can honestly say I never saw personified. You can feel the late adolescent bravado in the photos, his big goofy, toothy smile as he leans up against the feral pack of his Army buddies, cigarette dangling from the corner of his mouth, all rolled up jeans and wide collared, leather-jacketed libido. Standing in front of the Eiffel Tower and the Coliseum in Rome on various rail adventures from his Army post in Germany. My father in Paris, that's the man I have always longed to know. The man who I never got to meet. The man who died years before the coroner's van pulled up to the assisted living center to make it official.

During one obligatory holiday pilgrimage, I asked him about a photo that I unearthed from the box of black and whites, him standing in an amorous embrace with a comely blond woman, with staged tulips and windmills in the background.

"Oh, her? Yeah, that's the girl I knocked up."

"Whaaat—? When? How?"

"Well, if you have to ask 'how' then you got a problem, Bobby. I was nineteen. Wanted to marry her and bring her home. But she wouldn't. And I sure as hell wasn't going to live over there."

He resisted any kind of follow up conversation. My temples pulsed as the romantic in me imagined my father frolicking in clogs through the tulips, holding baby boy Gottfried or Hans in his arms. Or running into my adult half-sister on the streets of Amsterdam, recognizing the unmistakable genetic markers of buck teeth and square jaw and soft chin of the image of my father in drag.

"Would you pass the mashed potatoes, Bobby?" interrupting my reverie. "Whaaat?" he whined as I hesitated, my mouth agape and my hand resting on the bowl of spuds. "The potatoes, genius."

I've avoided the tempting delicious Dutch streets and alleyways on my travels to Europe and regrettably have missed out on that particular reunion with a half-sister or half-brother. I still long, though, for that man, the wild feral one who smoked too much, drank too much, and told me in a just-buzzed enough drunken haze of honesty about bedding another Dutch woman while her husband watched and took pictures. The one whose wily charms apparently no Dutch woman could resist.

Where did that one go? And why didn't he come back? And what was the journey like? I want to pick up the phone, to have the conversation that we never had, nor ever could. I am awash in the throes of midlife, fathering three boys, trying to partner with my wife, showing up at a job that provides for my family but often feels like punching in and punching out, passionless at times and then filled with infinite possibilities of taking on the world and telling stories and having Edward Norton play me in the movie versions of my various pithy memoirs yet to be written.

I miss my dad and grieve the things that I said to him before he died, trying to shake and startle life into him, a selfish act to help me appreciate my place and my being in the world. I am angry about the man that he was and sad about the man that he could never become. I worry that his patterns, forged across generations, reveal themselves as I rage against my boys, my beautiful boys whose only sin was to be born into a lineage of broken men. Still, I hope. I hope for a different way of being, of being father, husband, citizen…man.

Did he have these hopes, longing to be different, to be transformed? Maybe he did, and I missed it. Not knowing is the tragic part. Did he spend as much time thinking about all of this as I do, gripped with anxiety at 3 AM, staring at the ceiling regretting what I may have said to my boys or to my wife in anger, worrying about the mortgage bill that is a few days overdue, or the constant pulls on my soul from unfulfilled dreams? I long to be free from the narrative of a fatherless child, of the victim of his abuses and earnest but clumsy attempts at demonstrating love. I long to be informed by the past, known, and unknown, that haunts the various strands of DNA inhabiting and expressing in my own genome and that of my boys. Which of these traits are inevitably part of my essence, chosen or unchosen, and which ones can I change? In my lifetime or my boys' lifetimes.

Again, Paul Tillich captured this dilemma sublimely, "…infinite freedom expresses itself in two elements that belong to man at every moment, in a constantly unstable balance of anxiety and courage…Man's being accepts his anxiety, does not attempt to deny it, or overlook it but on the contrary does what the word 'courage' means, namely says 'Yes' to being despite the threat of nonbeing."

Somewhere along the way, my father said no, burying the threat of nonbeing, as unconsciously, perhaps, as I buried his ashes. Or more accurately, he ignored the conversation altogether, neither saying 'yes' nor 'no,' rendered inert and imprisoned by an unnamed fear that could not be spoken in the lonely hallways and dark corners of the structure of being a man during his lifetime.

My father let go.

And I hold on. That is all I can be responsible and accountable for in my own lifetime. Like Jacob in Hebrew scripture, I wrestle with the unknown, the dark Angel of God. With sinews strained and stretched like piano wires pounding out an unnamed requiem under the lid, I cleave to the angel through the night, resisting the pull to surrender and standing fast against the weariness.

Various scholars and experts of midrash have shared their interpretations, of wrestling with psychological angels and demons alike, of Jacob's tumult with Esau over a stolen blessing, and even of Jacob wrestling with Yahweh Himself. As with these sublime ancient and archetypal narratives, the story is a screen that I get to project all of my own angels and demons, my own sins of omission and commission, my own longing for blessing. So, I hold on.

And I implore my father, "Don't you let go."

For me. For him. For my boys. Don't let go.

As I dream, I receive the blessing, the balm for my wounds that I've refused to let heal. The angel, my father, God…all are gone, but not absent. I have my blessing, but I've also been touched at the hip during the fight. I walk away with a stilting limp, an ugly but obligatory wound across my hip that I know will scar down over time. It is a generational imperative it seems, like my grandfather's wooden leg, and my father's arthritic hip worn by time and both accidental and deliberate traumas. The wound will smooth and even recede out of my consciousness but will persist nonetheless, a stubborn but sacred reminder of the embrace.

I hold on.

Chapter Five

There remains within us a part of the original oneness that longs to return to that great spiritual reality from which we came and about which we have forgotten.

Donald Kalsched

My wife never stood a chance, either. Dreams of little girls prancing around in sundresses with pigtails bouncing in the wind have been deferred to a toilet seat perpetually in the up position, the floor drizzled with drops of pee from an infinite number of wayward shakes, and all sorts of sticks and fingers fashioned into play guns, despite the best intentions of my three boys' pacifist parents.

In a twist of cruel and delightful irony, the Herzog men have only gifted the world with male offspring, little Y-chromosomes swimming in a deep pool of Iron City six-packs and the amber hues of cheap whiskey. I was oblivious to this fact when I asked Xochi to marry me, for I would have at least been compelled to share the notion of my redundant arsenal of one-trick pony sperm. She was already concerned about our capacity to procreate, having married later in life, with her aging collection of eggs and my potentially slow-swimming sperm beset by boyhood years of tighty-whitey underwear and a gene code spliced by a regular supply of cheese puffs and Burger King Whoppers.

I called my father soon after my firstborn, Silas, was born. Before I could even get out the blessed news, he interrupted, "Well, what's *his* name?"

"How did you know it was a boy," I queried, resentful that I hadn't been able to share the news first about my little bundle of joy's fun parts.

"What the hell did you think you were gonna' have? It's always been boys in our family. Aw, shit…"

"Shit?! *Now* you tell me?!"

"Here's your mother," he interjected, having reached his usual threshold of two-minute conversations.

"Mom, did you know about this, did you think we were going to have a boy?"

"Well, of course, I did, Bobby. We already bought him a Stillers onesie," pronouncing the name of the hallowed black and gold NFL franchise in quintessential Pittsburgh-ese. I shook my head, as I passed the phone to the new mother, having reached my own usual threshold for three-minute conversations with my family.

Research shows that the odds of having another boy are stacked immensely in your favor once you have two boys, affirming the Herzog genealogical imperative. Still, after having produced another wonderful boy, Ezra, from the fruit of our loins, we waited expectantly for our third little one with girls' names at the ready. Our delightfully mystical, hippie and low intervention-loving midwife got our hopes up when she first reported that this baby's "energy was clearly feminine."

When our third son, Arlo, was born, gently moving into the waking world like a sulky Coltrane melody in the buttery dawning light of an early New Mexico spring, my wife looked up in immediate post-natal delirium and implored, "Does *she* have a penis?"

The odds of having a girl would have reverted back to fifty-fifty with the potential advent of a fourth child, but we were out of bedrooms in the house and frankly out of energy, raising our little brood in the weary throes of our late thirties. While there are emotional and financial perks of raising children later in life, they are frankly trumped by the evolutionary wisdom in birthing them in your late teens when your mind is bursting with delusional freshness and your knees are swimming in robust synovial pools of cartilage.

Having boys was splendid, filling me with unlimited springs of pride and visions of hitting them grounders, teaching them to shave and sharing the oft-shadowy secrets of the clitoris. Raising them terrified me. It still does. I long to do things differently, to raise little sentient beings who can be compassionate in the world while turning a wicked 6-4-3 double play on the baseball diamond. Yet as my parenting proceeds I recognize recycled generational patterns of rage, sadness, and exasperation. I grieve that I may be raising them awfully similar to how my father attempted to raise me.

I can remember my desire to have children from a preternaturally early age, and the fantastical visions were consumed by little boys, smiling and innocent and earnest as they ran through sun-kissed meadows, jumping lovingly into an unseen father's arms, just outside the frame of my technicolor dreams. This image would end with this fantasy father lifting the little boy to the azure sky, to the heavens, as if coveting a blessing.

Imagine my shock when I came a across a real-life, 3-D version of my vision, in full bronze cast, towering over the grounds of the Martin Luther King Museum in Atlanta, Georgia. The sculpture was of an African man, sinewy and powerful, holding his infant son in gentle caress within the crucible of enormous supplicant hands, longing for something, for everything for his young son. The child was wrapped peacefully in the comfort of swaddling clothes, so its sex was unclear. But I knew it was a boy. It had to be a boy.

I was on a summer mission trip with my youth group, a repressed high school senior-to-be doing good for the poor and dry humping with my girlfriend across the deep south and toward the occasion of sin. We were making our way from Jackson, Mississippi after having built a house with John Perkins' Voice of Calvary Mission, assuaging the unconscious guilt of our white privilege while fueled by the Gospel and Dr. Pepper. We made our way into Atlanta to spend the night with our youth group leader's family on our way back up the East Coast in our righteous white Econovan.

It was logical then and wonderfully earnest for the trip leaders to divert our itinerary towards the King Museum after our education in civil rights, poverty, and racism in the rural, impoverished haunts on the outskirts of

Jackson. The lessons I learned certainly ran deeper than the sociological or even the spiritual on this suburban to urban odyssey. I recall the wave of emotion that washed over me when I first saw the sculpture in all its profound glory, blinking away the tears that sprang from the depths of years of constriction and tightness in my saved soul. This was the stuff of wonder, of being touched by a universal truth that overwhelmed my still-developing sense of identity.

Behold, the sculptor Patrick Morelli titled the hulking and profound mass of iron and soul that towered over the magnificently white-tiled hallowed grounds of the museum, the hot Georgia sun reflecting off the tiles like undisturbed snow. The ritual celebrated the birth of the child, the father offering the child to God, to the universe, to himself even…behold, the only thing greater than myself. It seemed a prayer, a supplication, or a desperate cry for help, the father lacking the naturally imbued hormonal imperative to care for the new bundle of joy, unique to mothers. My 16-year old self-identified with the child, longing to be raised up, to be cared for, and to be held in such a tender and reverent gesture. My 50-something self identifies now with the father, projecting a remarkable admission of a mix of pride, love, and abject helplessness, "I have no idea what the fuck I am doing. Can someone, anyone, out there help a brother out?!"

The sculpture was masterfully mounted in place, its occupation of space an indelible narrative in its own right. It looked out toward the Ebeneezer Baptist Church, where both Martin and Daddy King reverberated from the pulpit, a legacy of father and son celebrating and invoking the Father and Son, summoning justice from prophets of old and inspiring new ones. King's tomb beckoned from just to the side of the sculpture, holding the new warrior father in a dignified profile, sublimely unaware of the joys and the sorrows that await both he and the child. The cherubic visage of the newborn in full view, himself oblivious to the sacred and profane history of the father that summoned him to this sacred precipice of manhood. Both entirely helpless and both carefully held in remarkable cosmic freedom above the fray.

"Free at last, free at last, thank God almighty I'm free at last," the stone mason's capable hands chiseled onto the pristine marble tile of King's tomb. The possibility and hope of a new life, ascending toward the heavens, held in the trembling comfort of a father's grip. The inevitability of mortality, descending toward the dust and Georgian clay.

The depiction of father and child also speaks to the unimaginable traumas suffered by both, grieving the tragic history of Africans sold into slavery and the even more tragic contemporary enslavement of the African American culture. Slave owners, both Southern then and neoliberal now, recognize the power of the relationship of the father to the family, especially the bond between father and son. Each has engaged in a measured and strategic removal of the father from the family to the heavy hands and whip of the slave owners then and to the heavy burden of modern ghettoes and police states and unjust mandatory sentence policies now. It is sacrifice of fathers and especially of our sons, the mournful and tragic opposite of raising them up.

Such filicide occupies a consistent and vexing part of our cultural heritage, revealing the timeless mythic truths in the tragic immediacy of parents taking the lives of their children. We turn away in revulsion and judgment at the stories of mothers ravaged by post-partum depression who drown their innocent infants, or at fathers who shake their babies to the point of irreparable brain damage or even death; we react with blame-the-victim disdain at the cultural filicide of our young African American men like Trayvon Martin and Michael Brown at the hands of paternalistic abuse of forces commissioned to protect and serve; but we fail to understand or even entertain the larger archetypal forces at play.

The Oedipus complex is bandied about in psychoanalytic circles, the phrase acquiring a dulling symbolic interpretation in our cultural lexicon. We would be served to face the abject horror of the roots of the story in Sophocles Theban's plays: King Laius, fearing the prophecy of the Oracle at Delphi that his son would grow to murder him, pierces his son's feet, and binds them so that he cannot crawl away, and leaves Oedipus exposed on the mountain to die. Only by the mercy of the shepherd assigned to deliver him to the mountain is Oedipus saved. In fulfillment of the prophecy Oedipus returns to the scene of the crime as a grown man, unwittingly perpetuating the generational violence. He encounters the Sphinx, literally "the one who binds" or "the one who strangles," stopping all travelers on their way to Thebes and challenging them to solve her riddle or risk being killed and eaten. Her riddle is the challenge of time and mortality, "What walks on four feet in the morning, two in the afternoon, and three at night?" Oedipus answers correctly, "Man, who crawls as a child, walks upright through midlife and leans on a cane in old age."

For his reward, he is made king to the widowed queen, Jocasta, spreading the violence throughout the family and throughout Thebes as drought and pestilence grip the city and violence binds Oedipus' heirs, including his daughter Antigone. Like Oedipus, we unwittingly participate in perpetuating familial and cultural violence, fearful of the inevitable death that awaits us at the hands of our cruelest offspring, the linear concept of time, the devouring force of Chronos. We search for a vector, a perceived deliverer of our fate, upon which we can project our fear and hate in consuming violence. It often comes in the form of those who we choose to subjugate, in chains literal and symbolic, or assigned to barbarians who wait at the gate, a collection of marauders beset on our demise, challenging our entrenched and sacrosanct "values" and "way of life." We respond at times with genocide and holocausts, veiled behind manifest destinies and cleansing utopian visions buttressed by latent misguided philosophies or the voice of God, Himself.

Hebrew holy writ spins its own cultural interpretation of the mimetic narrative in the story of Abraham and Isaac. Abraham heeds the call of God to sacrifice his son in the Book of Genesis, "Take your son, your only one, whom you love, Isaac, and go to the land of Moriah and offer him there as a burnt offering…" The incredulous and anxiety-provoking narrative is often spun easily as a testament to Abraham's faith, the commitment to his beloved God beyond all commitments, to sacrifice that which is most precious to honor the God beyond preciousness. The persistent and compelling nature of the biblical narratives rest in their marvelous, insightful, and often vexing reflections on the very nature of the soul, of the soul of man and indeed the soul of God. The story may offer a window into the very soul of relationship between believer and God, between the emerging self and the all-consuming and all demanding Other—the betrayal that is sewn into the fabric of the relationship between father and son, expressed throughout generations as sins of the father inevitably and universally visited on his sons.

Abraham is recorded as inextricably silent in response to the call for the destruction of the most sacred earthly covenant between parent and child, demanded from this God who promises covenant with Abraham and his heirs. The voice of God may simply be a projective expression of the betrayal that Abraham and his brother, Haran, had experienced at the hands of their own father, Terach, a viral replication of generational violence that runs rampant in the retelling of the lives of the patriarchs. Again, Genesis records "…Haran died *in the presence* of his father Terach, in the land of his birth, Ur of the Chaldeans (Genesis 11:28).

Jewish scholar Avivah Gottlieb Zornberg provides a remarkable reflection on Rashi's midrash commentary in her brilliant book, The Murmuring Deep: Reflections on a Biblical Unconscious, "…the essential fact is that Abraham's brother was *killed by his father*, who had originally intended Abraham's own death. By handing him over for execution, Terach is virtually, killing him. And when he is saved, his brother's actual death is directly attributable to Terach." Zornberg goes on to attest that there is trauma as the root of the relationship between Abraham and his God which "strains the very concept of fatherhood." This trauma is merely a perpetuation of the betrayal that Abraham witnessed in the death of his brother at the hands of their father, the betrayal that he had experienced himself.

Abraham has learned the fundamental lesson of history: That fathers betray their sons, having inherited this genetic imperative from generations of abuse. Christian scripture contains a similarly abrupt and oft-redacted theme at the center of its retelling of the story of Jesus's crucifixion, as he cries out in betrayal to his Father God while suffering the ultimate indignity of death for his faithfulness, "*My God, my God, why has thou forsaken me?*" The terror of that abandonment is often skirted during most Sunday morning homilies and sermons since it speaks to the existential state of anguish that most of us inevitably experience during various emotional and psychic traumas.

Psychologist James Hillman writes that at this precise moment, in recognition of the breaking of the primal trust between the son Jesus and the Father God, the *puer* aspect of God dies. As defined by Hillman, the *puer* is the character of the eternal child found in the masculine identity, the character who must experience a rite of passage into manhood. Redemption, salvation even, is only to be found when the transcendent innocence of the Divine passes through the gauntlet of betrayal and becomes human. This is the "masculine mystery" that Hillman describes, identifying betrayal as an essential characteristic of the relationship between fathers and sons.

Most cultures, especially indigenous ones, have their young boys participate in rites of passage in order to delineate the transition from boyhood to adulthood. The boys are allowed to experience the separation and estrangement that is the hallmark of all ritual, endure the trials of the ritual and then most importantly are welcomed back into the community. This is the hero's journey written about so eloquently by the beloved teacher of cultural myth, Joseph Campbell, and the story arc of every celebrated narrative from Homer's Odysseus to George Lucas's Luke Skywalker. Often these rituals involve some time of physical scarring as a means of breaking through the stubborn omnipotence that most adolescent boys cleave to in their puer stage of development. The wound is made sacred though as the entirety of the experience is held in liminal space, a threshold of holiness outside the normal bounds of cultural convention in which the participant is compelled to entertain the very forces of life and death. The old must die and the new is born again, with the newness welcomed and celebrated in a raucous and celebratory return to the community.

Our religious institutions once held the sacred responsibility of these rites of passage into adulthood, but have ceded the responsibility, or at least domesticated the wildness of these important transitions. The adolescent boy, not afforded the opportunity to experience this wildness, will seek out his own rituals, often through tattooing or sundry piercings, or even to the extreme circumstance of gang initiation.

If not initiated, the boy will become acculturated into something—a gang, the military, the corporate structure—in an endless quest for something bigger than himself. What role does the father play in this profound time of transition? Is it integral to the role of father, perpetuating the mystery of the masculine as Hillman describes, to risk betrayal with his son? A multitude of stories exist, both sacred and profane, even canonical, that extol the narrative of father and son, with the father inspired to filicide, symbolic or actual death of the son. Prophecies to kings and rulers and heads of families seem to confirm the inevitable passing of time, rendering the father, once all powerful, merely a passive participant in the raging course of time and fate and eventually death. In panic or at least a pervading sense of helplessness, the father will devour the son. Chronos, the Greek Titan God of Time, devours his children.

Abraham, and in a way my own father, were each engaged in a mindless recapitulation of generational violence, participating in the sacrifice of their sons in a schizoid sense of faith in an all-knowing God or in the insatiable force of time that demanded a sacrifice. The justification for such well-intended but often abusive and violent acts can be strong, whether it be interpreted as Abraham's unfaltering faith in the face of God's test or as an expression of an archaic "for your own good" ethos. And not just personal but cultural, as prevailing forces of power insulate themselves from losing that power by sacrificing fathers, imprisoning men and sons and brothers to the whims of unjust sentencing laws, to the soul-squelching pursuits of the corporate structure, or to the promised freedoms of ever-increasing violence of ultra-conservative political ideologies.

Isaac's story has a different ending, thanks be to God, redeemed in a liminal space of ritual and remembrance. The narrative unfolds in dramatic fashion as Isaac inquires of his father, "My father...behold the fire and the wood, but where is the lamb for the burnt offering?" I cannot begin to imagine the dissonant horror of the father, as he climbs the path to the summit of Mt. Moriah, availing himself of the possibility of taking his son's precious life, the life that the father is created to honor and cherish and protect. He responds to Isaac's question, "Here I am (*hineini*), my son. God will provide for Himself the lamb for the burnt offering."

Abraham, himself, had begun this arduous journey after having been sought by God, "Now it came about after these things, that God tested Abraham, and said to him, 'Abraham!'" And Abraham responded, "Here I am" (*hineini*). He is thrust immediately into alerted consciousness, as he responds similarly to both his son and to God, Himself. Abraham is caught between the radical present of his son, the beautiful life he had been blessed with and watched grow toward this precipice of manhood, and the all-powerful voice of God, calling to him from the past across generations of patriarchs, outside of time.

Still, Abraham persists and prepares the altar to fulfill the voice's call for sacrifice, unsure whether it is God's voice or his own. Isaac lies defenseless, bound and innocent on the wood laid deliberately over the stone altar—wood and stone that he must have collected earnestly with his father in the hot sun. He must look incredulously upon his father, eyes transfixed, heart beating, muscles and sinews stretching and struggling against the force of the binding ropes, against the forces of violence cascading powerfully down the winding river of generations. Abraham must be drawn to lock eyes with his son, his beautiful boy, but also resist his son's gaze in a fit of shame that he has allowed himself to be placed between heeding the call of the Past, the call that he understands as God's, and the Future that lies before him and before his generations in the presence of his dear son. He holds the knife above his future, fingers sweaty and tight cleaved around the hilt of the blade, arm trembling, eyes tightly shut anticipating the resistance of skin and muscle and bone to the thrusting force of metal blade, to the release of steel into his son's heart. Release from the voices that demand such sacrifice.

"Abraham!" The call shakes him to the core, the unwitting electrical impulse from his mind to the muscles of his arm and shoulder resting on the threshold of insufferable action."

"Abraham!" The call comes a second time, softer.

"Here I am," he responds, unsure of the source, looking around the sand and stubborn shrubs of the mountain top through the blur of teary eyes. It is the angel of Adonai, the messenger who summons Abraham, startling him into awareness, freeing him if only for a moment from the tragedy of squelching the spark of his son's soul.

"Here I am!" he responds, gratefully if not vexingly. Again, responding with *hineini*.

Abraham changed in the lull between the two calls. He can now truly hear and internalize the authentic nature of the message, calling him to understand the memory of the Past and not be victim to its whims demanding sacrifice. The essence of the message is for healing, not destruction;

for redemption, not perpetuation of generational violence; for raising up, not sacrifice.

As Avivah Gottlieb Zornberg remarks wonderfully in her recitation of Rashi's midrash, "God answers Abraham, 'I shall not profane My covenant and the utterance of My lips I shall not change. When I said to you, 'Take your son…' the utterance of My lips I shall not change: I did not say, 'Slaughter him,' but 'Bring him up.'"

God, his own voice, the voice of the Past—whichever it was, called Abraham with *ha' aleyhu*, which Abraham heard in its idiomatic interpretation, to sacrifice. The literal translation of *ha'aleyhu* is to *raise up*. Abraham heard the powerful and seductive voice of the Past to sacrifice his son, to consume him before Abraham was to be consumed, an act of self-preservation forged in the crucible and the ovens of sacrifices of generations of fathers and sons. And it has always been fathers and sons in my family. For my father, and his father, and who knows how many fathers before that.

And for my sons.

Abraham is alerted mercifully to a ram, caught in the thicket by its horns, which can satisfy the Past's call for blood, for sacrifice. Not so lucky for the ram, but of great fortune for Isaac and for Abraham. Zornberg comments from her study of midrash, "And Abraham lifted up his eyes and he saw—behold!—a ram—behind (*achar*)…*Chazor l'achorekha*—Turn around! Look behind you!" Abraham is summoned to examine the past, not just to look behind him with a spatial construct, but simply behind (*achar*).

And what a blessed reprieve to be able to reinterpret the past, to resist being seduced into repeating it. I have called you not to sacrifice, but to lift him up. Abraham can and does create a new narrative. He releases his perplexed and stunned son from the ropes that have bound him on the rudimentary and rough altar atop the mountain, embracing him with exhausted muscles, a quivering heart, and an unanticipated freedom to love. Father and son are changed, not healed magically, but changed to go forth from this holy place with the blessing of a changed heart, of a changed narrative. Abraham and Isaac are free to forge a new story, for themselves and for the generation of fathers and sons and daughters and wives to come after them.

The very thing that bound Isaac on the altar and bound Abraham to raise his knife, the horns of the ram bound in the thicket, are now momentarily redeemed, and carry the promise and possibility of generational redemption. The ram's horn is blown ritually, stubbornly, every year at the end of Yom Kippur as an expression and celebration of atonement. The restorying, the telling of the Future, is begun in the process of atonement, reflecting on the past but not being bound by it, being made free to write an original and complicated narrative, separated for but a moment from the tendrils of the past and its call for blood.

The shofar is sounded by the breath of these wonderfully complicated and fallible human beings, fallible fathers, fallible sons. Fallible but hopeful. What lies behind Abraham, Zornberg expresses, "…is the future of his past, the once inevitable consequences of those traumatizing messages; and a dynamic possibility—that his children, like him, will work to transform and translate the enigmas of their own past. This is God's offer: the perpetual return of the shofar cry, for memory and transfiguration."

We remember and we dare to transform.

Chapter Six

Spiritual reality-divinity enters into earthly matter to initiate a new sacramental creation.

Bruno Barnhart

The dear, brave mother or our boys has endeavored to bring our children to the world without the aid of epidurals, enduring unimaginable levels of pain engaging the liminal forces of death and dying while participating in calling forth new life. Our second son Ezra slid gently into a warm pool of water in a makeshift inflated pool at our home in Albuquerque, poking his head out to test the waters before gliding into our family. Arlo, our third, was born almost effortlessly (stated cavalierly by the adoring, attentive father) in that same bedroom in that same home. Xochi achieved a certain level of soulful comfort with home births, and had we extended our family to a fourth child she would no doubt have championed the cause to give birth in the great outdoors, chewing on redwood bark with various woodland creatures encircling her.

The first birth was not necessarily so gentle and easy. I have worked for over thirty years with children with disabilities, watching the sublime physical and emotional struggles of families whose births went horribly wrong. Xochi had lobbied for a home birth, but my professionally induced paranoia made us compromise for a birth-center experience, nestled comfortably across the street from a Level-II trauma center. My excitement in becoming a new father was tempered by visions of intubation tubes and NICU incubators so I wanted to have all of my bases covered.

As new and earnest parents we consumed as much information as we could get our hands on, reading books technical and spiritual, *What to Expect When You're Expecting* to *Birthing From Within*. We took birthing classes, breathing rhythmically, and promising blissfully to cultivate our relationship while Xochi leaned against me in various practice positions, and I held a handful of ice cubes for as long as I could to approximate her pain. And as new and earnest parents, all of that information flew out the window of the Bryn Mawr Birth Center as soon as the first contraction coursed through my wife's body, sending shock waves rippling toward the antiseptic confines of the hospital just across the street.

Xochi spent almost two days in labor, bouncing unceasingly on a birthing ball, shrieking in pitches high enough to pierce the ears of all of the dogs in all the houses on the Main Line and groaning low enough to summon the dead from their graves, while I exchanged panicked glances with our midwife at how long it was taking. She writhed in impossible levels of pain as Silas, our first son, decided to do somersaults in the birth canal into a posterior position, as they say in the birthing business, his soft spine grinding excruciatingly against his mother's spine. We had an earnest birthing plan which stated cavalierly that Xochi had wanted to stay at the birth center as long as possible, eschewing pain meds and hospital visits unless it was absolutely critical. But like the erstwhile philosopher, Mike Tyson famously stated, "Everybody has a plan until they get punched in the mouth."

Xochi's parents had joined us for the birth, anticipating a Rockwellian vision of babes in swaddling clothing and warm grandparent embraces. What they got instead was pissing, shitting, and puking and awkwardly observing their little girl writhe in agony. Xochi's mother was valiantly at her side, holding her hand and whispering encouraging words and singing hymns gently in her ear. Her father was in the birth suite's living room, eating an Italian hoagie from the deli next door, and watching the Knicks-Sixers game. And I remained helplessly at her head, wiping sweat from her brow, bearing the weight of her exhausted body to allay her anxiety, and cracking stupid jokes to comfort my own growing concern.

And none of it worked.

Xochi was a warrior, and our midwife was remarkable, trying every trick in the birthing book to get the boy out. She suggested that I move into full-blown nipple stimulation—of Xochi's nipples not mine, to be clear—in an attempt to increase natural oxytocin levels and to encourage her body to resume contractions that had stalled out from utter exhaustion. There is nothing natural, however, about feeling up your wife in this manner in front of your conservative, Jesus-lovin' mother-in-law. I rubbed until her nipples grew raw, despite various creams, salves, and incantations to make the process gentler. I don't think Xochi has forgiven me, making above the waist foreplay a bit more complicated.

We men are problem solvers to be sure, and now I was faced with the ultimate helplessness, staring into the abyss of this unsolvable problem, as the woman I loved suffered in anguish and the child that I might grow to love even more in potentially serious danger, if not fighting for his life. All of the facile spiritual metaphors of birth and death that both Xochi and I had delightfully bandied about in the nine months up to this critical juncture were now subjugated to the moans and shrieks of the transition phase of birth. Xochi was operating in a different space and time, of *Kairos*, while I wrestled anxiously in *Chronos* time, counting the agonizing and expanding minutes between stalled contractions.

Before having descended into the haze of dimmed but sublime consciousness Xochi made me swear to her that I would not concede to the short ambulance ride to the hospital and the magic of pharmaceutical relief for her pain and for my burgeoning anxiety. I tried to read the face of our midwife, being careful not to have Xochi read the anguish on my own face, and I was growing more alarmed as the midwife's brow furrowed more and her casual tones of conversation devolved into short bursts of firm, serious and staccato commands. I listened intently, long past the traditional male birthing roles of boiling water, ripping sheets, or pacing a white-walled waiting room, chain smoking my anxiety away. I helped to move Xochi's almost limp body into various positions, in an earnest attempt to massage her uterus into contracting just a few more times. The baby was not in distress. Not yet. But Xochi was, and I was getting close. She shook her head violently, asking me to make it go away, convinced that she could not do any more. I held back the tears of helplessness, working to exhibit the strength and fortitude my burgeoning family now demanded of me.

I held her face in my hands, with as much loving force that I could muster, from a place and depth of feeling that I did not know existed, "You can do this, and you will do this. There is only love."

I'm not sure what that last line even meant, but it served to move the process along, as the child we would know to be Silas inched down the birth canal to his loving but exhausted parents. The midwife, capitalizing on this moment of will, declared, "This is the last thing we. can try. If it doesn't work, we're taking a trip across the street, folks."

This desperate time called for desperate action, even superhuman.

As a wee lad of junior high age, I was enamored with the wrestling stylings of Jimmy "Superfly" Snuka, a taut, muscle-bound Samoan with an unruly shock of curly hair that bounced violently while he bounded from rope to rope in the wrestling ring. His signature move was dramatically mounting the top rope in the corner of the ring, high above the canvas, thrusting his arms out into the anticipating air before superfly-ing onto his unaware opponent lying prostrate on the ground.

Mr. Snuka had nothing on this spritely, sinewy dynamo of a midwife.

I can't remember much about her own maneuver, as the parts of my brain responsible for memory and clear thinking bowed to the evolutionary imperative of the fight-or-flight mechanism. I do recall a shadowy, ninja-type figure in flowy clothes moving to the head of the bed and launching in midair toward my wife's mid-section and the next moment hearing the most beautiful cries I had ever heard. Silas had arrived, a Stargazer they call the babies born face up, his eyes cast toward the heavens in unexpected and innocent anticipation. Xochi and I burst into grateful and exhausted tears, flowing from a place of unknown depth, as we held this beautiful and messy boy in our embrace.

He had made me a father. And the pride and fear, delight, and anxiety were just beginning.

Xochi's parents cooed and sighed at their new grandson. Ruth, Xochi's mother, brought over the birthday cake that she had been unassumingly crafting in the kitchen of the birthing suite, replete with a "0" candle and fresh Lancaster strawberries adorning the wonderful collection of carbohydrates and sugar that I gratefully ate up.

We stayed at the birthing suite for a few hours, as mother was tended to, cords were cut, the boy measured and weighed, and the father slapped on the back with a multitude of "'Atta, guy" congratulations. I loaded up the car, the 4-door sedan having realized its full family-transportation potential, bundled the boy up to face the early spring night chill, helped the exhausted mother to the passenger seat, and this new and wonderful family headed home on our trek down the Schuylkill Expressway toward our Art Museum-area brownstone. Silas kept sneezing throughout the drive, making me want to turn the car around and head back to the Birth Center or to the hospital, convinced that he had contracted a nasty virus, even Ebola, in his few short hours of life. One quick call to the midwife allayed my fears, as I discovered that it is indeed quite normal for babies to binge sneeze in order to clear the snot box of various fluids acquired during the birthing process.

I held this delightful new creature in my arms as Xochi methodically stepped her way to the third-floor bedroom, plopping into bed and bringing the boy to latch, the two of them in perfect repose, my own private Holy Family scene come to life. It wasn't long before they both surrendered to sleep in the comfort of a billowy recline under the loving warmth of homemade quilts of purples and pinks. My fatigue had surrendered to a hyper-vigilant state of wakefulness, a remarkable remnant of the evolutionary imperative of millions of fathers over millions of years, attentive for threats from hungry saber tooth tigers to the hungry ghosts of generations of family traumas.

I futzed and putzed around, unloading the diaper bag and reviewing the various vibrant hues of baby poop on the chart that the midwife had gifted us on our way out the door. I stacked more cloth diapers on the changing table and stared at Xochi and my new son for any number of minutes, hoping that they might wake up immediately and hoping that they could sleep for days. Luckily, I spied the congratulatory cigar that friends had purchased for me. Rousing my brother-in-law's neurotic Vizsla, Oliver, from slumber, I tied his leash on and dragged him out the front door, grateful for his tail-wagging company. I fired up the cigar in the expectant chill of the late spring, starry night, imagining my little Stargazer son orbiting around the gravitational pull of his mother's slowly beating heart.

Remembering the little bodega that might still be open around the corner I pulled up the collar on my jacket, hopeful that I could still score a gallon of milk for a bowl of celebratory cereal in these wee hours. The cigar gave me something to concentrate on as I pulled rolls of smoke into my mouth and billowed spent miasmas of smoke and the vapors of my cold breath into the dark night. I meandered mindlessly in the direction of the corner store, having never meandered quite so much in my pre-fatherhood days. After finally arriving at my destination, I plunked down an indiscriminate amount of money on the counter for the milk, unable to do the basic math of my purchase, buying the world's only twenty-dollar gallon of milk outside of the food lines of Communist Russia.

Oliver and I walked a few blocks when my meandering came to a screeching halt, the dog sniffing at the night air for the reason that I had stopped so abruptly.

"I have a son," I mumbled quietly with determination under one of the early blooming cherry trees that adorned the narrow neighborhood streets.

"What the fuck am I doing out *here*?! I have to get *home*...." That last word landed in a hearty thud in my gut as I took off in a full sprint down the street, completely out of my mind. I ran the four blocks at an Olympic-worthy pace, my heart pumping and my legs churning, even running a hundred feet past my block. I skidded to a stop, leaving Chuck Taylor skid marks on the cracked sidewalk, reversing my path, and flying up the three flights of stairs. I climbed up the last few steps in deep, panting, panicked breaths, finally calming myself and my abrupt arrival on the landing as I slowly opened the door to peek in on the family unit. They hadn't moved an inch as their deep, tired breath moved in sync.

After my heart descended from my throat into its rightful and now hypertrophied place in my chest I reached down and carefully lifted my son from his mother's tender grasp. I snuggled him deep in the crook of my elbow and gently laid another blanket on the length of his already burrowed body. Descending the creaking stairs as carefully as I could in the early morning dark, I made my way on to the front sidewalk under a bright waxing moonlight, backlit by the silvery row of streetlight serenades. The spires of moss-covered gray-green walls from the old Fairmount Prison provided a backdrop at the end of the block, silhouetted against the deep black-purple hues of the night sky. Without particular knowledge and profound history of the gesture I slowly lifted the boy, this new life untouched and unburdened by the various vagaries and joys of life, into the sky lit by the urban glow and stubbornly bright stars.

I lifted him in joyful prayer.
I lifted him in surrender.
I lifted him in grief.
I lifted him in hope.
I lifted him up.
Behold, the only thing greater than myself.

I made my way back into the house, perhaps both of us fundamentally changed by this recognition and celebration of father and son, bound to one another in something entirely random but something also entirely fated . I laid him in his mother's arms and watched as his tongue rooted reflexively for the simple and profound delight of milk, responding to the smell and to the warmth of her safe embrace. Retracing my mindless steps and mindful recognition, I found Oliver a few blocks away, leash lying uselessly at his paws, licking up what was left from the spilled gallon of milk, my cereal plans extinguished. The cigar lay on the ground, stubborn embers still glowing. I lit the end of the cigar, watching the smoke from the match ascend to the flickering bright glow of the cityscape.

And I returned home.

Chapter Seven

When love has carried us above all things, we receive in peace the Incomprehensible Light, enfolding us and penetrating us. What is this Light, if it be not a contemplation of the Infinite and an intuition of Eternity? We behold that which we are, and we are that which we behold; because our being, without losing anything of its own personality, is united with the Divine Life.

John van Ruysbroeck

My second-born, Ezra, has never been quite sure about this world. Big-hearted and old-souled, tinged with a melancholic streak, and a tad cynical, he is often disappointed in how things go in the world—or at least occasionally disappointed with his father. I should have known about his personality from the first moment I met him.

I knew it before I met him, having lived with similar romanticism, longing, and melancholy.

The family had moved from our earnest row home in the quickly gentrifying Ukrainian neighborhood in the Philadelphia Art Museum area to a parcel of land in the South Valley of Albuquerque, complete with golden leaved cottonwood trees, irrigation ditches snaking from the Rio Grande River, and neighbors who were eager to teach us Spanish. I had accepted a job with the Center for Action and Contemplation, founded by iconoclast and spiritual guru, Father Richard Rohr.

The property served as the first meeting place for the CAC under Grandfather Cottonwood, the noble and majestic tree that towered over the property. The previous owners had been active in the sanctuary movement of the 1980's, housing refugees from the tumultuous Central American civil wars. It seemed the perfect place for our burgeoning family to hunker down and participate in our romantic visions of what the world could and should be.

My wife and I had married late and were intent on growing our family before biological clocks intensified in their ticking, so Xochi's pregnancy annunciation heralded soon after we had landed and unloaded the boxes stuffed into the nooks and crannies of the moving van. Our crew of three would soon expand to four, five if you include Gus the Wonder Mutt, a chow and Pitbull mix who opted for the warm confines of our house over his life as a street dog begging for scraps. He fit right into our ragtag collection of strays, prophets, and witches.

Fittingly, we eschewed a hospital or birth center process for Ezra and the family, instead squeezing a large blow-up pool into the small bathroom just off the master bedroom, the warm waters welcoming our baby boy into the world. Except he wasn't so sure about leaving the cozy confines of his mother's womb. The labor was long and arduous, as only a man can describe in minimizing detail, but not as violent or dramatic as his older brother's labor. My wife was a warrior once again and after hours of bouncing on therapy balls, singing incantations, and lying in the warm tub while I rubbed her back and shoulders, Ezra was crowning his way into the darkness of the New Mexico early morning and its welcoming waters.

Ezra's head poked out to assess the situation, discovering the outside world oddly similar to the amniotic realm of his mother's womb with a view. Instinctively, I wanted to pull him out and get him to safety above the water, worried that he was drowning. The midwife assured me that our little fish was breathing fine, with nature's wonderful SCUBA gear on board, the intact umbilical cord providing everything he needed to move from one aquatic environment to another. As I would come to know him in the coming years, he decided that he wasn't quite certain about the world he was observing, so he darted quickly back into the safer confines.

We all just gasped. And then laughed at our little aquanaut. He eventually conceded and floated into waters filled with the delightful murkiness of birth fluids. He wailed as he drew his first breath above water, his lungs resonating with the wonder and power of our oxygen-filled atmosphere. He still wasn't convinced.

He's struggled to find his way, to find his tribe. Sometimes our family is that tribe. Sometimes, not so much. He has objected to his parents' hippie sensibilities, preferring the more suburban "modern" housing over our 100-yr old country property, longing for wall-mounted flat screen TVs over reading fairy tales and gnome exploits. He rejected the Waldorf Charter school education that took us from New Mexico to the mecca of public Waldorf education in the North Bay of San Francisco. He decided instead to migrate to the big public school and its big-time athletic program, having sprouted to six-foot-four and basketball and baseball prowess. He lived in the tiny house that he had built with his mentor for his eighth-grade project, coming into the main house mostly just to eat or shit.

And then COVID hit, the schools shut down, and he was disappointed in Zoom classes and disinterested and overwhelmed public-school teachers. And then he broke his leg on a breakaway in the final game of the fall basketball league right before varsity tryouts. So, he quit. I had to get over my own stigmas about having a high school dropout, explaining to inquisitive friends and family that he quit, but assuredly, that he "had a plan." Ezra is my entrepreneur, dreaming big dreams and holding expansive visions. My wife and I have joked that we will lament our horrific, hippie parenting when he becomes wealthy and running a successful company, "Where did we go wrong?!"

He hunkered down and studied doggedly for his high school equivalency certificate, cramming four years of information into one exam, including the dreaded math that he hadn't ever been taught. I honestly did not have great expectations when I roused him from sleep on a cold wintry morning and dropped him off at the district testing site with the other disgruntled misfit kids—the stoners, the goth kids, and all the other kids too anxious to be in school. And my Ezra.

The results would take months to be processed. He could pass one section and then re-take the other, which is what I had anticipated, given his distaste for all things algebraic and geometric. When that fated envelope arrived in the mail, I hesitated to hand it to him, aware and fearful of the fallout from another few months of math tutoring. He passed, eking out the math section and flourishing at an unexpected but not altogether surprising ninety-something percentile in language arts. He almost immediately began signing up for classes at the local esteemed junior college, matriculating into their entrepreneurship curriculum.

Such a worthy accomplishment deserved a worthy celebration. Two of my three boys are baseball fanatics, having been reared along the foul lines at Albuquerque Isotopes games, collecting foul balls and bobbleheads for their bedroom shelves. They've witnessed the San Francisco Giants run of three World Series titles in five years right after we moved to the Bay Area, going to sleep with stories of Buster Posey's earnest exploits, Tim "The Freak" Lincecum's no-hitters, and Brian Wilson's torturous relief outings behind his unruly, dyed beard. All slightly different than their father's long-suffering fandom of his hometown Pittsburgh Pirates and nostalgia for the "We Are Family" days of Willie Stargell-led and coke-fueled World Series championship in 1979.

Ezra's phone has an app that tracks all of the major league parks that he has been to, hellbent on seeing them all. Trips to cousins' cities have afforded him the opportunity to attend Washington Nationals, Houston Astros, and really good seats at the barely attended Florida Marlins games. Summer travel ball tournaments to various major league cities have checked off Dodgers and Diamondback parks off the list. But he hadn't been to the cathedrals, the meccas of baseball fandom, Wrigley, Fenway, even Camden Yards, the first of the wave of intimate parks that replaced concrete behemoth ringed parks like Three Rivers Stadium and Veterans Stadium that went the way of demolition and replacement. I might even put Yankee Stadium in there if the Steinbrenner bastards hadn't given up the original for a bright, shiny new vacuous version.

I offered him a free pass to any of those parks, a just reward for all the work that he had put into his studying process—to the victors go the spoils of peanuts and crackerjacks and not caring if we ever got back. And

I had my own selfish motives, wanting to forge these father-son memories in the context of this beautiful game that had greased the skids for father-son conversations when there was nothing else to converse about. As Daniel Stern's character remembers in the film "City Slickers," "When I was about eighteen and my dad and I couldn't communicate about anything, we could still talk about baseball. And that—that was real." Maybe we could still talk about baseball and experience that sublime collision with the Real.

Instead of choosing those hallowed destinations—which are still on his list and mine—he chose PNC Park in Pittsburgh, the gorgeous riverfront park that was the only balm for the diseased state of the Pirates organization through years of losses and apathetic and overwhelmed ownership groups. It offers a gorgeous view of the Pittsburgh city scape, nestled in between the golden bridges spanning the Ohio, Allegheny, and Monongahela Rivers.

"I'd rather see the Pirates and get to see where you grew up, Dad," he stated simply as his father listened to the profundity with gratitude in his heart and certainly tears in his eyes. This big heartedness is the authentic identity of this beautiful boy, shining through the customary adolescent gruffness and apathy.

By the time plans were made, it was right before the end of the regular season, so I hustled through searches for last minute, expensive airline tickets, harried Airbnb reservations, and stabs at secondary ticket markets. We would catch the Pirates against the St. Louis Cardinals and venerable slugger Albert Pujols' last regular season games with the Cards and then drive a couple of hours through the imminent fall beauty of the Ohio landscape to Cleveland to catch a Guardians game and check another park off of the list.

We hunkered down at our Air BnB in the Mexican War Streets, a wonderfully odd and gentrifying neighborhood on Pittsburgh's historic North Side, within walking distance from the ballpark. A trip to my hometown city would not be complete without a visit to Primanti's to savor the haute cuisine of sandwiches brimming with French fries and coleslaw pushing out of the sides of the bun in carbohydrate glory. We dined, we enjoyed Iron City beer from the can, and lit up victory cigars for our walk to the game. We talked about baseball at first, regaling my boy with stories of the 1979 World Series Pirates squad, the batting lineup still fresh in my mind from Omar "The Antelope" Moreno to Willie "Pops" Stargell to Ed "The Otter" Ott, the squat, no-hit, all-glove catcher who platooned with that other squat, no-hit, all-glove catcher Steve Nicosia.

The conversation morphed, as it can infrequently when the adolescent haze clears, into his plans for college and his life philosophies, the furor of COVID shutdown and its consequences, the latest young woman he was chatting up, although he resisted his father's wily charms and advice on wooing women. We sat at the riverside park just outside the stadium, puffing away on cigars, taking in the ubiquitous Pittsburgh hills and fresh gold paint on the Roberto Clemente Bridge. It was heaven. In Pittsburgh. Two words that I don't often place in the same sentence.

I might associate the two more frequently if it weren't for the persistent memories of my family. It's a wonderful city, mostly undiscovered and unknown to me, having ventured to college at 17 and never looking back for fear of turning into a pillar of salt—or at least a pillar of cigarette ash given my parents' smoking habits. My son was quickly redeeming those memories, redeeming this city as the game progressed and the sky over the right field wall lit up with the early fall sunset framing the skyline. The game was eventful—Albert Pujols did hit that final home run of his hallowed career, even drawing a standing ovation from the respectful and thin crowd at the park. The Pirates even managed a rare win, aided by the wildness of the Cardinals closer, walking the bases loaded and then walking in the winning run on four pitches.

We walked back to our condo, mostly in silence amid a bit of persistent jet lag after a big day. Ezra broke the comfortable silence, "I really appreciate you bringing me on this trip, Dad." His earnestness was indisputable, the sincerity oozing out of every pore, rarified time, and space between adolescent and expectant father. "I'd love to see where you grew up."

Where I grew up. The idea of having grown up made me chuckle, evoking a deep cough from the cigars and the low-grade cold that both of us had brought with us from California. My mother had just sold my childhood home, fetching what seemed to me a remarkable price of

$135,000 for all 1,165 square feet of high pile carpet, kitschy furniture, and cigarette-stained ceilings. The real estate pictures of the staged home on Clay Drive made the place feel even smaller than I had remembered it, despite the realtor's attempts to show off the place with photographs taken with an earnest wide-angle lens.

The photos were taken on a bright, sunny day with the drapes open and the walls lit up. I only knew the place in its dark and shadowy usual expression, my mother preferring to keep the curtains drawn and all the lights off, warming only with the eternal glow of the television while she slept restlessly on the living room sofa. She would stir and mutter, scolding anyone who tried to turn off the TV, "I'm still awake, goddamnit!" She did not often sink into a deep sleep, hovering just above disorganized alpha waves, born out of years of having to be quickly reactive to the emotional duress and threats of violence that occupied her home. I often sleep with the same fragile consciousness, stirred by the simplest of sounds, an owl hooting in the distance, the dog stirring on the couch that he's not supposed to sleep on, the teenagers coming home late at night rummaging through the refrigerator.

We climbed into the rental car to make the trip to the first ring of working-class suburbs east of the city. I had scored major adolescent cred at the rental car garage when the attendant pulled up in a Smurf-blue convertible Ford Mustang. Despite the obvious marker for mid-life crisis car rental absurdity, the car was the cheapest one available, our reservations made at the last minute. Top down, heater on, sweatshirt hoodies donned, Juice World blaring on Spotify connected to the bitchin' car stereo, we made our way.

We passed the remnants of riverside industry, rusting old steel mills and empty warehouses, interspersed with newer buildings, shiny new steel and glass and intellectual capital bursting from the seams and gutters of green roofs, foreboding hospital buildings rising from the hills as the University of Pittsburgh Medical Center continued its technological manifest destiny through the last remnants of available building space, and the county jail perched over the river, the one my father lamented having his tax dollars channeled to make criminals' lives soft. "They got a goddamn better view than I'll ever have."

The Mustang revved as distant muscle memory managed the turn from the Parkway to the Rodi Rd. exit toward Penn Hills. We passed the Stoneledge neighborhood, what passed for fetishized upper middle-class homes with families with college degrees and two cars parked in fancy double garages—the neighborhood Mr. Marshall referenced in AP English while he sang aloud the line from The Great Gatsby, "The Stoneledge Rich get richer, and the Poor get children!" Past the bus stop where kids shivered in the maw of Pittsburgh winters in snow boots with grocery bags stuffed in the bottom to keep small feet dry and warm. Where I earned the purple and black badges of courage on my skinny legs, lugging the baritone case from my house to Dible Elementary band practice, my dreams of playing the trumpet like Chuck Mangione deferred when my mother discovered that the band needed a baritone player and would rent the instrument to us free of charge.

I parked the Mustang on the estimable slope of Clay Drive, enlisting the parking brake and turning the wheels toward the curb like the Driver's Ed teacher had drilled into our heads during summer lessons. The stories that Ezra and his brothers insisted that I tell and retell when they were little and still revered the wisdom of their old man began to make more sense when Ezra got out of the car and looked down the looming depths of the street.

"Oh, now I get it...this is where you rode sleds in the winter trying to kill yourselves. Crazy." My fellow neighborhood hellions and I would stage a contest of bravado, riding our sleds down the snowy hill whenever a car started up the hill, counting the houses before we had to bail out into one of the yards before being serving as a speed bump to the oncoming car. His words, though sparse, were music to my ears, longing for him to understand just a little bit what it was like to grow up rockin' the suburbs in our enclave of Italian, Irish, and more Italian families. I could remember more easily now, his lanky frame and earnest soul providing a generational buffer and even a conduit between me and those days I'd tried so diligently to forget.

Ezra was remembering. Remembering for him. Remembering for me, allowing me time and distance from things that felt immediate and unbearably close at times. Close, loud, and evocative. He was remembering for my mother, for my father, for our ancestors. He didn't even know it.

He was remembering with one simple statement that spawned this very trip, "I want to see where you grew up, dad."

I have felt bound to these memories and the full expression of emotions that they evoke, creating a feedback loop in which the tumult and the havoc have been experienced over and over again. The feelings are neither integrated nor worked through, rather the trauma is reinforced and perpetuated—with the goal of healing tantalizingly just beyond my reach.

In Greek mythology Perseus stole fire from Zeus and offered it to humanity. For his transgression, Perseus was sentenced to be bound to a rock for eternity while having his liver eaten by an eagle each day. Perseus's liver would regenerate through the night only to have the eagle return to eat it once again. The Greeks believed that the liver harbored all human emotion. Emotions are evoked, consumed, and then regenerated, only to be consumed once again. I have known this exhaustive cycle and longed to be done with it.

I may have needed a warrior to help me become unbound. In Hesiod's retelling of the myth, Perseus was freed by the great warrior, Heracles, he himself from the paternal lineage of Zeus, Perseus, and the god of ecstasy, madness, and pleasure, Dionysus. The Romans adopted the narrative of Heracles, renaming him Hercules.

Hercules, the namesake of the missile system that my father trained on, the tool of war but also the tool of seemingly noble defense.

John David Herzog, Jr. My father. Hercules to a young boy. Herk, as he was known to all.

My Ezra, who, out of my three boys bears the closest resemblance, through both soma and soul, to the Herzog line. An emissary for my father. My teacher. My warrior hero who helps me remember, who helps to release me from the eternal punishment, unbinding the strong man through his strength.

The Herzog family home had been sold so I didn't feel entirely comfortable knocking on the door, explaining to the new owners that the realtor hadn't declared that their new backyard contained the remains of my father. We walked next door to the orange-bricked house where the Long family used to live, paint chipping and front yard overgrown, compared to the other manicured lawns of the neighborhood—it looked abandoned and provided easy access to where I had buried my father's ashes as we walked along the cracked mosaic concrete of the driveway framed by rusting and fallen down gutters.

The leaves were holding on to their green, patiently awaiting the full splendor bloom of a remarkable Pennsylvania Fall. There wasn't much to see, buckeye saplings and various pines pushing their way toward the canopy of trees that shaded the backyard of that house. That house. There were remnants of the backfill that my father had pursued to try and extend the backyard—old, decaying pieces of wood, the rusty pole from the basketball hoop that hung in the back driveway, an old section of chain link fence. Ezra and I stood in silence, an awkward reverence hanging in the thick air of memory. Memories that my son knew second hand from stories told around campfires and family dinners, now filling in with first-hand experience of the ground, of the clay, mud, and dirt that stained the knees of Tough Skin jeans of my youth. And had stained and informed my parenting of him.

After a little while, he looked at me with compassion and understanding that belied his mere seventeen years hanging around this earthly realm. I was grateful to have him see this hallowed ground, to witness the full range of emotions evoked in remembering my father. To engage those memories through the filter of his soul, softening my own anger and allowing a new path to engage the grief that had been buried right along with my father's ashes. He may have gained a more nuanced understanding of my parenting, born in the crucible of my father's despairing violence. I felt a little more forgiven. I felt the grace he extended. I felt the grace that exists all around us, like water around a fish, the sacred milieu that is unveiled if we have eyes to see. I saw that grace through Ezra's eyes.

We drove to the top of the hill, the revered flat ground that spanned three or four houses in length, just enough space to host our games of tackle football on the macadam, inspiring yelling, and calls to the police from Mrs. Mazzei and the other neighbors when their cable programs were interrupted by the football battering the overhead wires. Rich DeFazio throwing tight sunlit spirals with his rocket arm.

I showed him my old high school, walking around the football filed as he generously listened to stories of my football glory days, the 51-yard

Hitson to Herzog aerial that won the senior homecoming game against McKeesport. Making out with spritely cheerleaders after dances. My parents showing up under Friday night lights, buttons with pictures of their thinly mustachioed son proudly adorning their winter coats.

We made the obligatory stop at Pizza Palace, the shop opened by Frank Pasqualino who lived two houses from me as a kid. Frank would come home every night with a brown paper bag filled with cash and a gun resting on top to protect the hard-earned fruits of his labor. Frank's boys, Vince my first and best friend, and Damiano had an Italian restaurant empire throughout various Pittsburgh suburbs. And they still had the best pizza ever made. We feasted on the squared slice cheesy delight while we made our way to Seneca Place, just down the road.

Seneca Place is an expansive campus created as an homage and final resting place for aging Boomers, a one-stop shopping of various buildings with various levels of care for folks on their journeys to the end. The campus used to house Seneca Junior High School and the field where I began my football exploits as a skinny, bow-legged offensive lineman with the Penn Hills Braves at age eight, my father's attempt to toughen up his sensitive son. It's where my dad showed up every night for five years, without fail, to watch my practices. Where we would climb into the car after practice on the way to Timeout Tavern so my dad could have a shot and a beer.

My father always showed up. And then he would always disappear.

Seneca Place was also where my father died. He was transferred back to the skilled nursing facility when my mother could no longer care for him at home while on hospice, as her fear of the inevitability of losing him slowly consumed her already-limited emotional capacities.

She had moved into a brand new, antiseptic, uber-tiled senior independent living apartment just down the road from Seneca Place, a way-station for the impending transfer to more skilled care. She still wasn't speaking to me for what I had said to my father before he died. Despite my repeated attempts to offer apologies and seek forgiveness. It was easier for her to forget, the memories of my father and her hostile dependency on him still too painful to conjure.

My mother participated in forgetting. Because remembering was just too hard for her. She had been born out of wedlock in France before the

Occupation, bad timing to be a bastard child. My grandmother never told my mother who her father was, she was of the generation of assimilation and never had spoken about the horrors of wartime. My grandmother, Granny Grace, was quite a looker back in the day. She made the unfortunate choice to slap the Nazi soldier who was flirting with her, ending up in a hard labor camp for an extended time before France was liberated. She hitched her wagon to an American GI, Walter Junker, like many did in these swirling post-war family narratives. My mother stayed with her grandmother while Grace was in the camp, eventually offering to raise her, since Grace was not interested in parenting. Grace declined the offer, and she and my mother expectantly boarded a ship for the US, their eventual destination, the American Dream city of Pittsburgh, Walter's hometown.

Grace and Walter divorced fairly soon after, as many of those post-war marriages sputtered upon reaching the shores of the American Dream. But not before Walter would leave his violent imprint on the family, battering Grace and sexually abusing my mother. So many of our family narratives are born in the same crucible of violence and abuse. They are never spoken of, in polite or impolite company, while the resulting pain and perpetuated violence leak out. Grace battered her daughter, my mother, senselessly, unable to understand and find redemption from the abject violence she experienced, the narrative of the violence cobbled together out of forgetting through whispered family stories, tattered black and white photographs, and imagination to fill in the gaps. God knows what stories were harbored even deeper in the family psyche.

My mother endured beatings from her mother for years, eventually finding herself exiled at the age of sixteen, forced to find a job and her own cramped, decrepit apartment. When asked about the violence that she visited on me and my half-siblings, she would comment, "Well we hit you, but we never beat you." Grace beat my mother. The truancy officer from my mother's school eventually intervened and they were reunited until Yolande continued the family legacy and got knocked up at 17, scurrying off to Maryland for a shotgun wedding that was still illegal in Pennsylvania.

Forgetting was more convenient for my mother, the gatekeeping strategy to keep those painful feelings locked away, though as Shakespeare reminds us in Macbeth, "The grief that does not speak whispers the o'erfraught heart and bids it break." Or as that other erstwhile philosopher Kanye West, reminds us, "Hurt people hurt people."

Grace made her way through several more marriages, outliving some of them, divorcing the others. She eventually moved in with my mother and father for the last ten years of her life. My mother chose, or was compelled, to take care of the woman who had beaten her, shamed her, kicked her out of the house to fend for herself. I cannot even begin to imagine the emotional furor swirling within my mother. So, she forgot. She made an active choice not to remember.

Grace eventually withered away, her skin flaking off from years of steroids to combat the horrific rheumatoid arthritis, her fragile body collapsing in on itself in self-destructive terror. Forgetting. After Grace died, my mother stayed up all night, moving all of the furniture out of my grandmother's room to the street for garbage pickup. She even repainted the walls, in a desperate attempt to exile the memories from her mind and from her soul.

Forgetting. When my father died, my mother threw away all of his old uniforms, the kitschy Steelers paraphernalia, his stacks of Military Modeler magazines tucked away in the corner of the unfinished basement, the shadowbox of his military medals that were his pride and joy. All of the things that I wanted to rummage through, to feel, to smell, to conjure up and sustain memories of the man that I hardly knew.

She even had the dog, Toby, the constant presence that never left my father's side, put down. Because it reminded her of the grief, and pain, and loneliness. The vet handled those remains, so Toby was not afforded the dignified burial that other family pets and my father experienced.

Forgetting. After I made my father cry that fated day on the porch, my mother would have nothing to do with me, with me having committed the unpardonable sin of blaspheming the man who had saved her. The man who adored her, drove her crazy, bowed to her power and authority, and even redeemed the image of men. I had attempted to make amends through efforts grandiose and small, including multiple phone calls to offer apologies and seek forgiveness. She would have none of it. Most of the time, she would not answer the phone and I would hang up or leave a snarky voicemail message that I knew she would never hear. Other times, she would miss the caller ID, answer the phone, hear my hopeful "hello," and then grunt "Aaaach" and immediately hang up the phone.

Forgetting. Ezra and I stood in the lobby of the senior apartments, trying to find the phone code for my mother's apartment. I eventually found the code and entered the numbers with an enormous pit in my stomach at the potential embarrassment in front of my son. She answered the buzz in her apartment.

"Hey, Yo, it's your son and your grandson."

"Bobby?" she replied shakingly. "Whaaat," she exclaimed. And then she hung up.

We ducked through the second door of security, having been given ample time as one of the senior denizens of the apartment complex wrangled her walker with the ubiquitous worn tennis balls guarding the wheels through the tight confines of the entrance. We made our way to her apartment on the fifth floor, the new tile floors and freshly painted walls still glistening earnestly as the dull Muzak played through speakers. We knocked furtively on the door, as I raised my eyebrows and shrugged my shoulders towards Ezra, standing behind me at this door to memory. She opened the door slowly, the shock on her ageing, wrinkled face offering an odd satisfactory blessing on the strange odyssey from California to the welcome mat in front of my mother's door.

"What are you doing here?" she quizzed.

"Well, we were in the neighborhood…"

She hadn't seen Ezra since she and my father had visited us in New Mexico 15 years earlier. When the cancer that my father was denying had spread to his liver, framing his slate blue eyes in a pool of yellowed jaundice. Ezra had grown into a man by this time, filling his lanky frame with blond hair and his own remarkable blue eyes. He was a Herzog. She must have recognized something of my father in his face. And I recognized myself in my mother's face, despite the wrinkles, the sallow skin, and the deep sadness in her eyes. Or perhaps because of that same deep sadness.

The conversation began awkwardly, then settled into a flow of idle but light chit-chat. Of the new apartment, Ezra's remarkable growth spurt over the previous 15 years, the baseball-inspired trip to Pittsburgh. It was a conversation between strangers. Strangers with a common story, a shared bloodline, a universal narrative of memory and forgetting.

I made certain to get a picture of grandmother and grandson. As Ezra draped his arm sweetly and tenderly over his grandmother's frail and narrowing shoulders, I was able to see her in a different light. To see her in her full humanity, or at least the fullest I could imagine with the grief, anger, and shame still swirling between us. Ezra was colluding with the universe, to allow this unexpected healing. And the healing was and is fleeting, as it exists within a constant negotiation with the Real. It is a paradox of will and surrender to imagine a different way, to imagine restoration and renewal.

And the sublime possibility was interrupted by mother's wonderous earthiness, her constant buffer between her and intimacy.

She was never one to receive or give affection easily. Ezra's loving gesture was no exception. "Now don't you grab my boob, Ezra!" as his long arm hung over the narrow precipice of her shoulders.

She offered to take us out to lunch at Eat 'N Park, home of the Superburger Platter, withered iceberg lettuce at the salad bar, burnt coffee, and other sundry suburban Pittsburgh haute cuisine. I politely declined, content with how the visit had transpired with a sort of acceptable neutrality, deciding not to push our luck with more time.

More time.

More time to stumble toward forgiveness. More time to bear witness to my mother's aging, happening painfully slowly with newfound wrinkles and persistent stubbornness. More time to watch my son grow into a young man, that one happening more quickly, as he reaches his full height and broad shoulders of late adolescence and early adulthood.

It is remarkable to understand that time passes differently, based on evolving concepts of time and space that are worthy wrestling opponents for physicists and cosmologists, philosophers and theologians, young people hellbent on getting older and older people longing to be young. Time passes faster the further you are from the Earth's Center—known as gravitational time dilation, thanks to Einstein and his memory of the future expressed in wild-haired ideas and literal wild hair.

We clamber for the heights of purpose and accomplishment and first half of life grandeur while slowly and sometimes painstakingly making our way closer to the humus, to the center of the Earth in the sublime decaying of our bodies. We long for the resurrection of the Christ who was not to be found in the tomb, while our bodies resist resurrection in holy recycling and reconstitution into the wonder of micro-biomes. And along the way hopefully adding a dash of wisdom acquired during the aging process to enrich our families and our culture.

We reach the still point of being. As TS Elliot reminds us:

At the still point of the turning world. Neither flesh nor fleshless. Neither from nor towards; at the still point, where the dance is. But neither arrest nor movement…Where past and future are gathered. Neither movement from nor towards. Neither ascent nor decline. Except for the point, the still point, there would be no dance, and there is only the dance.

More time to remember. To remember who my father was and even dare to remember him differently than the reified stories that my pained and porous memory construct to fill in the gaps of unknowing and forgetting.

To bear a memory of the future that Einstein dreamed of asleep at his patent clerk desk in the wee hours of a bitter but ultimately forgiving Swiss winter dripping into glorious spring.

To remember what my future might look like, what my son's life might contain in the midst of superbugs and shutdowns and broken legs on basketball fastbreaks. All the disappointments. His and mine. Transformed. Redeemed. Made whole once again.

I worry that these sins, my sadness, and disappointment, have been visited upon him. And it almost seems more violent than my father's open-handed slaps, shaming sneers, and dismissive curses.

So, I show up for my son Ezra. I show up like my dad showed up, messy but consistent. And I hope that I show up one or two degrees differently than he did. I offer praise while being careful not to be that overbearing parent, I stay curious about his friends and his plans for the future. I am overwrought when observing his grief, muddled with my own. I cajole. I retreat when he is prickly, again muddled with my own prickliness. I try to see him while stubbornly and ungraciously withdrawing my projections on him.

I remember.

I remember his joyous howls when pulled from the water of the plastic pool on the day of his birth. I remember his beautiful smile, the glint in his eye when he would wave at every passerby in the grocery store when he was a toddler. I try to reconcile those memories with the present, with the challenging times that he and his adolescent cohort have endured through COVID-inspired anxiety and deep sadness of lives robbed of more typical blasé adolescent dramas—of zits and basketball tryouts, of boring high school classes and Homecoming dance invitations, of college applications and part-time jobs. All of it.

The Welsh have a hauntingly beautiful word, *hiraeth*. It is a sort of homesickness, a longing for a home that may have never been. It is the desire for a return to innocence. An innocence that may never have existed and certainly does not exist in the complicated crucible of the present. Still, we imagine, we insist that it not only exists, but that we may will ourselves back to it.

That innocent, romantic desire has had to run the gauntlet of experience, like all of our hopes and desires. Our hope for a more innocent time, made manifest in various circles as making things "great again," returning to a bygone era that may have never existed in the fullness that we remember. This is the profound and oft-maddening paradox, that we are already whole, already beloved, yet we have to go through experience—through betrayals and disappointments, through delights and successes to reach the other side—where we already reside.

This may be the elusive maturity that we seek, the autonomy that we resist mightily in our pursuit of that more innocent way of being and running from the movement into experience in all its messy glory. We resist change. We resist falling apart. Entropy is the unmitigated law of the universe. Things fall apart, things move from order into disorder and chaos. Yet there is order to be had in that chaos. Entropy need not be understood as mere dysregulation and chaos; rather, it can reflect the infinite number of ways that a set of objects, or even time itself, can be arranged. We exist in the realm of infinite possibilities because of the very essence of change, entropy, and decay that seem threatening to our instinct for order. Jesus and other wisdom traditions have reminded us that we have to "die before we die."

Otherwise, we are met by forces that fear both the real and imagined barbarian at our gates, sowing discord and rape and pillaging of our desire for order and even "our way of life." The Other. It thrusts into a sense of de-animation, a conservatism based on a notion of scarcity, that there will never be enough. Our very lives depend on it. So, we must hoard. Toilet paper and our own sacrosanct ideologies. We fly our "Don't Tread on Me" yellow flags from the safe confines of our gated communities and working-class enclaves alike. We long for a strong man, the archetypal protective Father, who will reinvigorate the once-glorious past, returning us to our manifest destined post as all powerful individuals. He will carry a Bible in one hand as he teargasses protestors with the other.

And we will believe him. The trains will run on time. The sanctity of a certain vision of marriage and education and individual rights free from "woke" culture will be restored. But we will be static, drowning in the same small ideological pool of brackish water. And we will assent to the very means of enhanced interrogation as the water from that small pool is poured into our unsuspecting, gaping mouths that had just previously been crowing about our freedoms.

We are heirs to infinite possibilities in each and every moment. If we are willing to risk everything, to hurtle ourselves into that ordered chaos without the promise of safety. This is not a paid endorsement for clean or uncomplicated living. For in those infinite possibilities is contained the gamut of bad decisions, angry reactions, sins of omission and commission alike. And the possibilities for joy and wonder, for just enough shame to bear our accountability and compassion, for order in and because of the chaos.

We may even choose to remember our past differently. Not a suppression of the past but a graceful bearing of it. To understand it, to metabolize it, to even learn from it. But not demand it be different, not to fetishize and wallow in our past hurts and resentments. To be more than a sum of our collective traumas, gumming up our gears in secrets and grudges. To be free enough to remember it in all its complicated, sharp-angled, vainglorious glory.

And we embrace it all, as messy and unruly houseguests as Rumi offers:

> *This being human is a guest house.*
> *Every morning a new arrival.*
>
> *A joy, a depression, a meanness,*
> *some momentary awareness comes*
> *as an unexpected visitor.*
>
> *Welcome and entertain them all!*
> *Even if they're a crowd of sorrows,*
> *who violently sweep your house*
> *empty of its furniture,*
> *still, treat each guest honorably.*
> *He may be clearing you out*
> *for some new delight.*
>
> *The dark thought, the shame, the malice,*
> *meet them at the door laughing,*
> *and invite them in.*
>
> *Be grateful for whoever comes,*
> *because each has been sent*
> *as a guide from beyond.*

Ezra and I woke early in our Airbnb, my back stiff from sleeping on the pullout sofa and my body weary from listening to my boy's fitful sleeping patterns. I spent an hour or three in the wee hours of the morning reading my book in the uncomfortable confines of the bathtub, longing for comfort buffering the cold tub with various pillows and blankets in my makeshift reading nook.

My trusty Smurf-blue Mustang steed awaited on the road outside the house. I breathed a sigh of relief to discover that it had not been broken into, rolling the dice on refusing the extra insurance offered earnestly at the rental car counter. We slung our suitcases into the narrow trunk, observed our breath in the cold Pittsburgh late fall as the convertible top retracted slowly, and made our way through the constricted streets toward the freedom of the wider road—the Turnpike that would seduce the driver of this blue beast to top speeds.

We drove towards a new town. A new baseball park to check off Ezra's list—with a banal, new corporate sponsorship logo writ large. A new team, the Indians having ditched their racist mascot for a nebulous Guardian, the figure perched in art-deco splendor on the bridge leading to the ballpark.

We drove west in silence. Towards newness. We drove west, racing the sun, toward the inevitable end of this day, the memory of it and days to come just above the horizon of consciousness.

We drove into chaos. Into order. Into possibility.

And even forgiveness.

Chapter Eight

The ethereal call that the future makes upon the present, that God's universe makes upon its current manifestation, is to strive to become present to the other as Thou and to make visible the unity and sacredness of all Being.

Peter Gabel

I found them accidentally at the bottom of an old box while rooting through dusty, unattended shelves. I chuckled as I held the ancient VHS football video tapes from the zenith of my athletic prowess when I was a skinny, bow-legged kid playing safety at Juniata College, a small Division III liberal arts school nestled in the woods of Central Pennsylvania.

Before my dadbod came to fruition. Before I made noises when I stood up and sat down. Before I started taking a fistful of Advils in advance of basketball games in the driveway with my boys.

Dusty labels, tattered, the writing on the front of the box faded from too many years and too many moving vans, I had no idea what they might contain. Still, it felt like an archaeological project that might unearth something revelatory, if not silly, as I waxed nostalgic for the glory days of my late teens and early twenties, of intact cartilage in various joints. Of skirmishes against obscure liberal arts schools dotted throughout the

Pennsylvania landscape—Widener University, Lebanon Valley College, and the fierce rivalry with the Susquehanna University River Hawks, among others.

I thought that the tapes might be able to bolster my case for reclaimed youthful exuberance, providing scant evidence to the stories I've told sparingly over the years about my gridiron feats—ones that usually evoked sustained eye rolls and adolescent "whatever" anthems.

I brushed them off, holding them with care to avoid damaging these relics from the bygone technical civilization of the Herzog Dynasty of 1986-1989, C.E. Do VCRs still even exist, I wondered? It would have been easy to end my quest there, chalking it up to the absurdity of a middle-aged dad hell-bent on capturing the innocence of past days of glory. I could even hear the Springsteen anthem lilting in the background, the Boss's under-bite belting out wonderful everyman lyrics of recapturing Glory Days.

Still, I persisted, imagining myself Parsifal in search of the Grail, Ponce de Leon bushwhacking through the swamps of Florida longing for the fabled cool waters of the Fountain of Youth, my father waxing poetic over the photos of his slim body and original teeth while stationed in the Army in Germany. I plopped down my $2.50 for the VCR at the local Goodwill and held this treasure to my chest with a sort of 1980's suspended animation, while conjuring up the spirits of Blockbuster video stores, the enticing smell of microwave popcorn, the smooth, fake satiny feel of Members Only jackets and the strange alchemy of Polo cologne and Aquanet hairspray.

The VCR had gone the way of all things nostalgic, rotary phones, Walkman cassette players, high top Chuck Taylors worn to Senior Prom. "What the *hell* is that, an iron lung machine?" my oldest son exclaimed as he observed me fiddling with various wires in hopes of resurrecting this archaic technology, my head tilted back, gaze turned downward trying earnestly to read the small writing of the input/output ports at the back of the television.

"Just help me get it hooked up, smartass."

With his young eyes and tech skills forged with ease in the crucible of interweb sensibilities, we had the ancient machine operating in a few minutes. Our Frankenstein monster of various parts and wires and spunk had come to life, animated by a stroke of lightning and noble, if not misguided, intentions.

The gaping jaws of the machine sucked the old tape from my hands before I could reconsider. The familiar hum of rotors and whirring of machine parts stuttered and then smoothed, as I even noticed a puff of smoke coming out of the back. The screen lit up, as my pulse quickened.

And then nothing but static.

No blue and gold reverie of Juniata Indian uniforms. No view of College Hill, or coeds spread out in their crop tops and Ray-Bans on blankets just below the orange brick at South Hall. No green grass and pristine white chalk lines on the gridiron at Chuck Know Stadium. No helmets scarred by battles along the line of scrimmage.

Just static.

And then I heard it.

"C'mon Bobby!" the voice echoed. That voice. Unmistakable in its throaty, high pitch, textured with the hack of excess—too many cigarettes, Iron City's, and shots of Jack Daniels.

I could hear the cowbell of Dan Crossey's mother ringing into the blue sky above Chuck Knox Stadium. My mother's occasional screeching. Mark Bremer's dad shouted along with my father, hunkered down on the cold, steel benches supporting the ample back sides of the Penn Hills families that were part of the recruiting pipeline that supplied the natural resources of sweat and sinew from western to central Pennsylvania. I imagined the grief of Mr. Bremer, whose son Mark, a thick necked exuberate linebacker, was killed in the line of duty as a Maryland police officer.

I felt my own grief at hearing my father's voice, almost ten years after he had died from cancer that riddled his body, his body finally letting go after a lifetime of his own grief, loss, and anger.

My heart dropped into my stomach, just like it had on game day on those beautiful, crisp fall days in Pennsylvania when the team made its way in rows of two, marching to the field with cleats clicking along the pavement in full expression of youthful bravado. That instant right before kickoff when nervous anticipation gives way to glorious and electrifying contact of helmet on helmet.

My son broke the silence. "That's so cool!" he exclaimed, a phrase I rarely heard in reference to me from his removed, adolescent snarky repertoire.

Tears filled my eyes, and I looked away, surprised and a little embarrassed by the effect of hearing his voice. Dad had been gone for almost ten years, but the sound of his voice still inspired a strange amalgam of fear and excitement, especially around the game of football. My dad loved and hated the game. Like most Pittsburghers, he would huddle in front of the TV on Sundays, hurrying back from Mass at St. Susanna's to worship his true idols, Bradshaw, Lambert, Harris, and "Mean" Joe Greene. He wore his lucky black and gold beanie, surrounding himself with full rations of Iron City six-packs and various snacks while sucking his way through a pack or two of those awful-smelling Winchester Little Cigars.

Steelers wins were good days at the Herzog household. He would once in a while even splurge for a pizza from Pasqualino's Pizza Palace for dinner.

Losses meant you found something to do outside, so you didn't become part of his Iron-City fueled wrath. "Geezus goddamn Christ," he would scream from the living room, hurling insults at whatever poor player who had dared to miss a tackle or throw an interception. He saved his most particular vitriol for Franco Harris, a bi-racial, eventual Hall of Fame running back from the Steelers who often danced out of bounds to avoid a bone-jarring tackle, efficiently fitting two slurs in one caustic comment, "Stay in bounds, you dumb (n word)-wop!"

It was no wonder then that he signed his only son up for the Penn Hills Braves at the tender age of nine, joining the local Pop Warner team before my half-sister could convince my mother to sign me up for the O'Steen School of Dance and infuse my straight hair with body-wave curls. Football always prevailed in this sports-crazed town, where fathers lived out frustrated dreams and left it to other frustrated coaches to toughen up their sons under the blazing scrutiny of Friday night lights and Saturday afternoon rites of passage.

One thing my father did was show up. He attended every practice of my Pop Warner career from the nine-year old days as a skinny, bow-legged center on the Braves to when I was a lanky, bow-legged center on the Bantams at 13-years old. The teams of all different ages practiced on the grounds of Seneca Junior High School, occupying different strata of the expansive field, earning different rank and privilege as they made their way up to the highest levels.

We ran laps around the gravel track upon making any egregious off-sides or worse yet, showed any kind of mercy to the lineman across from you. We were subjected to seemingly endless up-downs and bear crawl conditioning drills; had our prepubescent manhood challenged by post-pubescent man-child coaches; we learned lessons about grit and guile on The Boards, lining up across from our teammates and combatants in awkward three-point stances, feet splayed aside a long 4" by 8" wooden board—meeting helmet to helmet and shoulder pad to shoulder pad in 30-second trials of force and freneticism until we lie face down in the mud breathing heavily, inhaling fumes from the once-vibrant grazing lands unearthed during cold, fall Pennsylvania rains.

And it was exhilarating, hitting people without consequences. The shaming techniques of 70's-era coaching strategy were not much different than those we endured at the hands and sometimes the fists of our fathers. But we got to hit back. Not at perpetrators, but at least we got to hit at *something*, that something very much *someone* who served as the guileless recipient of all our rage. And we even got praised for it, learning to crush the will of the smaller and the weaker, in the service of gaining a few yards of territory and gaining the respect of our loudly vindictive coaches.

The coaches were tasked with the *loco parentis* role of toughening up "our boys," helping them cross the threshold from boy to man and growing into the athletic supporters and protective cups that hanged indiscriminately between our pre-pubescent legs. They worked to extend the lineage of manhood and masculinity forged in the crucible of a middling, lower-middle-class existence filled with frustrated dreams of their own, listless jobs and utilitarian marriages. Yet they also had a sort of awkward, earnest sweetness that reared itself during times of loss, the championship failure against the McKeesport Little Tigers, when they might put an arm around your shoulder, admonish you for crying and offer a hearty slap on the ass, "We'll get 'em next time, kid!"

My father escaped the fate of his mundane working-class stupor by showing up every night at every practice. He did shift work, so he was home by three and available to drive me in the two-toned black and gold Chevette to practice. He languished around the field with his dog, Frisky, a two-tone black and gold Yorkshire Terrier, walking laps or talking with other fathers over cigarettes and hopes and laments about this year's Steelers exploits. At the end of practice, shoulder pads and helmets were shed in the cold of a fall evening, revealing sweaty, wet t-shirts, and my father would let Frisky off of the leash, and the dog would run across the Seneca fields to find me. The dog would stop at the other big-eared and head-shaven boys until he found me, licking off all of the salty sweat from my brow as we rolled around together on the sparse grass. Those few seconds of frolicking contained the joy and freedom of being young, alive, and unbound.

Then he would shoot me a look. I always knew his looks, or at least was conservative in interpreting them for my own safety. This one meant, "Get your ass in the car. We got a 20-minute drive home and I'm cold, goddamnit!" or something similar to that. Yet we always made one detour, the prioritized reason for his presence, for his showing up. He would pull into the parking lot later at the Time Out Tavern on Saltsburg Road, between Fox's Pizza Den and the Stop 'N Go market. I remember so distinctly because I sat in the car fiddling with the radio buttons, smelling the sublime, pepperoni-smelling grease from the pizza joint before wandering down to the market on my appointed rounds to buy my father Tic-Tac's to cover the smell of the shot and beer from my mother's justified paranoia about his drinking.

I have such vivid memories of the day he invited me into the bar with him. It felt like entering the Holy of Holies, like I should tie a rope around my skinny, cleated foot like the high priests of yore, just in case they were consumed by the power of daring to encounter their gods. The bar was predictably dark, lit by the hues of neon Budweiser and Iron City Beer signs and the TV propped high in the corner with the incessant loop of Pittsburgh sports playing loudly. A strange glass jar rested on the corner of the bar, filled with vinegary brine and hardboiled eggs.

"Give the kid a Shirley Temple, or some shit like that," my father barked to the bartender.

"With a cherry in it, jagoff, or did he already pop it?" the bartender spit back, a deep-throated and Lucky Strikes-inspired cough bellowing with his laughter.

Their witticisms gave way to an awkward silence and the clarion ring of the register. My father pushed across two-dollar bills to me with a wink of his eye and the foam of the Iron City draft on his upper lip.

"Why don't you keep the change, Bobby."

It was a good day.

My feet dangled off the barstool, but my back was straight, and my nose tickled with the bubbles of the peculiar brown drink in front of me, the sweet and sugary nectar of the gods. The maraschino cherry burst deliciously in my mouth, as I chugged the rest of the drink, like I had seen my old man throw back the last few sips of his beer. It burned going down, but it was a redeemable pain for my newfound manhood.

He leaned over and offered me a Tic-Tac as he tilted the plastic container of mints deep into his own gullet, tapping the last stubborn few at the bottom.

"Now remember, practice ran late if your mother asks." I was never happier to be an accomplice in my father's deceit.

"You got it, shit-for-brains?"

My father showed up. Never muttering more than a few sentences to bark out orders or complain about my mother's nagging. But he showed up.

He and my mother would make the six-hour round trip on game-day Saturdays from the working-class ring of Pittsburgh suburbia along Route Twenty-Two through the rolling hills and valleys and fall colors surrounding the verdant countryside of Huntingdon, home of Juniata College. The routine was always the same—after the game, we would pose for a few awkward pictures as I rolled off the athletic tape from my wrists, and my mother would count the bruises on my forearms, clad with her Juniata Football sweatshirt and pin with my stoic uniformed picture and steely attempts at tough-guy bravado adorning the corner of the baggy sweatshirt. My father carried the ubiquitous clunky black case that held the shoulder-mounted video camera used to capture the shaky and often unfocused game film that resembled the Zapruder tapes.

They waited while I showered, chatting with the other faithful and cold-hardened parents on the field. We then scurried off to dinner at the Big Wrangler Steakhouse, adorning our trays with tough steak, French fries, and chocolate pudding, making our way past the buffet aisles. We would mostly eat in silence, and then return to my dorm room, sharing my mother's awkward attempts at good-bye hugs and my father's slaps on the back. My father was always eager to pick up a copy of The Juniatian, the black and white school newspaper that printed Mike Antenucci's game notes and statistics from the previous week's game.

They got back in the car and made their way home, taking turns driving while the other one slept. Honestly, like any other self-absorbed late teen, I forgot about them pretty quickly as I moved on to beers at whatever campus party beckoned and a fistful of aspirin to dull the pulsing pain in my back and knees from that day's game.

My father quietly kept all those copies of the Juniatian that I watched him casually pick up from the lobby of the student center. He diligently recorded his son's progress from unexpectedly making the travel squad as a freshman special teamer to sophomore starter to junior all conference, highlighting in bright, bold yellow my occasional mention in Nuch's Notes with an interception or tackle tally. He died a little when I skipped my senior year and football captaincy to travel further east to big city Philadelphia to begin graduate school early...it might as well have been the opposite end of the Earth to my old man. Without football, there wasn't much fodder for us to relate to one another. We could still talk of the Steeler's quarterbacking woes after Bradshaw retired or endless reflections on the weather and the bathroom habits of whatever small terrier dog occupied his consciousness. But things had changed.

I would still schlep the Pennsylvania Turnpike between Philadelphia and Pittsburgh, logging miles and the occasional speeding ticket from a slack-jawed state trooper during my holiday treks. But those trips became less frequent as a burgeoning semi-adult life beckoned my attention and interest. My parents didn't have reason to make their way east anymore, no pageantry of fall Saturday football skirmishes to drag them from their quiet, comforting routines. They came to Philadelphia for the big stuff... my wedding...the birth of my first son, but we fell into the habit of semi-regular phone calls with my mother mostly, as she would softly utter the hopeful phrase to me, "Do you want to talk to your father?" as she passed the phone to my father in mid-sentence.

Until I received the phone call from my mother that my father had been diagnosed with lung cancer. Now we had something to talk about. You would think. The cancer spread quickly, metastasizing from his lungs to his kidney and liver and eventually to his spine, riddling him with sharp bursts of pain that he endured stoically…with the help of ample doses of morphine. I can't seem to recall doctors having much of a plan to combat the cancer, no radiation or chemotherapy or other last-minute reprieves. I do remember that my father had been dying a little bit every day I knew him, so this news came as no surprise. I know that he was scared, though he dared not admit it, but it gave him a semblance of relief to finally let go for good.

He got sicker very quickly, descending into a haze of pain medications and oxygen bottles and fitful sleeps. The family, and mostly my iron-willed sister, quickly surmised that my mother could not care for my father at home. She could not remotely abide the notion of losing her husband, her whole life. Just the idea of such a loss, setting off a panic and fear that she had no emotional capacity to bear, sublimating her angst in middle of the night vacuuming, chain smoking and gulping down pots of bad coffee. Her hands shook and her eyes filled easily with tears when she spoke of my father in bursts of manic speech.

My father found his way back to Seneca Junior High, the place that was seared in his memory, though that memory was now fading quickly. Reflective of the demographic changes in our evolving, little working-class town, the number of school-aged kids had been plummeting and the number of aging boomers had been skyrocketing. And most of them were not aging well, like my father, requiring more beds and more sophisticated care. The property where the school lived for years, the halls filled with the ringing squeals and screams of pubescent boys and girls, the fields soaked with the sweat of young football heroes, was purchased by the leviathan University of Pittsburgh Medical Center to make way for senior housing, a skilled nursing facility and a hospice.

The property had been cleared for my father to die.

Red brick buildings replaced the bleachers where anxious parents had once sat on crisp Fall Saturdays, the buildings like Russian nesting dolls, moving down the developmental ladder from the nursing home building to the skilled nursing facility building to the hospice building. Pavement sat atop the holy ground where boys crossed sacred, and at times profane, thresholds into becoming young men. And now my father was crossing his own threshold, begrudgingly, from strength to weakness, from young to old, from father to ancestor. The descent had been obvious for as long as I'd known him in my own adulthood and fatherhood. But this was real. And final.

I didn't make it back before he died. He spent a considerable amount of time in hospice at home, the hospital bed occupying the tiny living room. He gulped down Turner's Iced Tea, watched the History Channel and pet his constant companion, Toby, a mischievous terrier that licked at the scabs on his hands from the IVs. My mother grew increasingly erratic as the prospect of my father's imminent death increased. She refused to give him the morphine that sat chilled in the refrigerator, fearing that she might get in trouble if she gave him too much. The dying process intensifies personalities and ways of being, exacerbated by the weight of anxiety, existential dread, and the fear of being alone.

My sister, who had nobly been overseeing the entirety of this process, swooped in from her post in Northern Virginia and demanded that the social worker have my father returned to Seneca Place for a 5-day period of respite. My mother could not bear to see her husband in that state so she would bound in for short visits, joking and swearing with the orderlies and the nurses as a way of skirting her pain. My sister did the yeoman's work of sitting at my father's bedside, bringing Toby for visits, and buying him more of his favorite iced tea and McDonald's, not sure which meal would be his last supper. My mother longed to wash her hands of the whole thing, even if unwittingly.

He couldn't go, worried about leaving my mother alone. He cried, wanting to see his own mother, Phyllis, who had died when I was a young boy. He adored her, and the pictures of them together were the only memory I have of him as joyful. As he slipped in and out of consciousness, he said that he wanted to go with Toby, his faithful companion, for fear that "Jesus would come and take the dog instead."

My sister called our mother, imploring her to get to the hospice before it was too late. She refused at first, but finally relented to my sister's dogged attempts. She came into the room, arm in arm with her friend Georgette, with take-out from Arby's, roast beef sandwiches and onion rings, the smell of which still haunts my sister's memory, as she stood aghast as witness to my mother's denial.

My sister made her spend time alone with my father, 30 minutes of what must have been excruciatingly painful for my mother to say goodbye to the only man who had ever cared for her, she a poor, abused bastard kid who emigrated from France after the war, fatherless and rudderless after her divorce from her first husband who had knocked her up at seventeen. They were each other's world, and no one could compete.

He died soon after, a peaceful letting go inspired by heavy doses of morphine to keep the physical pain at bay. He had let go long ago in response to the pain and disappointment that ravaged his soul. My mother had him cremated in Aspinwall, where she got the best deal, ever pragmatic. There was no funeral. No memorial. His life ended, and ours went on. My mother remained suspended in a de-animated, mournful liminal state. But that didn't stop her from cleaning out the basement, cleaning out all of the memories of him: throwing away the Army uniforms, medals and combat boots that he had kept pristine since his retirement; the model airplanes, fetid glues and paints and Military Modeler magazines that occupied his time in the basement throughout my childhood; the tools in the garage; the stacks of porn magazines that grew dusty in the garage cabinets, in the same spot that I had gleefully discovered them as a teenager; the box of family photo albums that had occupied a reverent place in the hallway closet for years; all of it…gone.

All of him…gone.

Yet one thing remained, the talisman that even my mother could not part with while rendered mad in the midst of her grief. My father had compiled a scrapbook of all my football exploits, from the picture of sweaty nine-year old kid playing center with a neck roll and smelly J-Pads adorning his skinny forearms to the football bylines from the Juniatian newspaper that he pocketed at every Saturday visit in college.

There were pictures and programs from the Youth Bowl we won in Cincinnati as 13-year-old Bantams; grainy newspaper clippings of a mid-80's Penn Hills senior with a silly, thin moustache and feathered hair announcing my recruitment; the announcement of the academic scholarship that I had won from his company, Mine Safety Appliance that he showed off to his co-workers during 15-minute breaks from his machinist station. There were even small, circular burn marks from the ashes that dropped from the Winchester Little Cigar hanging in the corner of his mouth while he sat hunched over the kitchen table. He had even pasted in a photo of the bleachers at one of my college games, the familiar guy at the end of the stands with the cumbersome old-school video camera resting conspicuously on his shoulder, the faded image circled in red Sharpie pen the size of a nickel. "See, I was here," the red circle invites the reader to know.

The same video camera that I loathed when he brought it out, pressing the button to have it whir into electronic life and embarrassing me in front of my girlfriend on the post-game field. The same video camera that produced the dusty, weathered tapes that I slipped into my thrift store VCR, catapulting me to a time when he and I were both a little bit more alive. For my sons, who were now just bounding with endless vigor. My memories could be their memories. And those memories could be good ones if I allowed them to be. Of a proud, imperfect man who showed up, sometimes big and scary, but he showed up, nonetheless. And that is to be celebrated.

And remembered.

I coughed up the considerable amount of money to have the VCR tapes converted to digital, incredulous that I could hold the profundity of all those memories on a two-inch USB flash drive. My knees and my back creak a little bit when I sit down at my laptop on my office desk, a reminder of all those bear crawls, sprints, and violent tackles, and climbing the steps of the bleachers to meet my parents after games. I squinted a little to find the right port for the flash drive, and in a burst of pixels, I am back on the field at Chuck Knox Stadium at the bottom of College

Hill. The sun is shining and the sight of me as a young man is intoxicating, along with the odd comforting sound of helmet against helmet and shoulder pad against shoulder pad. And I know that my father is somewhere in those bleachers above me.

I play the videos occasionally when no one is looking. Sometimes I close my eyes, waiting anxiously to hear my father's gruff, proud screaming over the din, "Way to go, Bobby!"

Chapter Nine

We die. That may be the meaning of life.
But we do language.
That may be the measure of our lives.
Toni Morrison

I stood at Guardian Rock, resolute and filled with both grief and appreciation, in the verdant Marin County hills high above the campus where I was taking classes toward my doctorate in psychology. I held aloft the small plastic baggie filled with a sprinkling of my father's ashes that I had saved from the metal box that now lay buried in the ground behind my childhood home. I breathed a sigh of relief when the ashes made it safely through the security checkpoint in the Pittsburgh Airport on my way home. Hoping not to catch the attention of an enthusiastic TSA agent, thinking I was sneaking a gnarly charcoal-hued eight-ball on the plane.

I held one of the bony fragments in the sunlight. I had expected to find only dust when I opened the utilitarian metal container. Instead, there were angled and pointy shards, with crags and crevices that once held the pulsing marrow of a life lived in hesitant poetry and prose. I tried to imagine this one stray fragment as part of a whole man, bones and flesh and sweat, and pride and shame. This fragment, reflecting the sun and refracting my memory, held a surface area that I dared to estimate.

What is the true measure of a man? How do we dare define what a "good" man is? We certainly can cite examples of men who have sinned, sins of violent commission and sins of cowardly, or at least ambivalent, omission alike. History is replete with men who have raped, pillaged, warred, abused, subjugated, burned, capitulated. And visited their sins upon the children. It is the history of mankind.

Yet we know of men who have defended, marched, protected, honored, encouraged, toiled, died for their brothers and sisters. And their children. It may very well be the true and essential history of humankind. Or at least its future.

And like most things, the real and honest measure of man contains multitudes and is hidden in a complicated alchemy of anger and kindness, of violence and waging peace, of madness and fragile sanity. It is the story of many, if not most, of our fathers. It is the story of my father, a man who stewed in unspoken grief and shame; in steely silence and flourishing fits of rage. And also a man who sacrificed, who stood fast and resolute, albeit wobbly in his role as man and father. He showed up. He persisted through the soul-draining monotony of his work in order to provide for his family precariously above the poverty line. He white-knuckled a perverse sense of sobriety while longing to drown himself in Jack Daniels, swigging nips at the bottle tucked away in the dining room with me as complicit lookout for my mother. She would sigh and shame him as she shook her head at the half-empty bottle of whiskey. That she had bought him.

His existence, his measure, remained bound between the historic imperative of the sins of *his* father and *his* father before him—recorded for posterity, and sense of will and sacrifice outside of time that has gone largely unacknowledged by historians and storytellers alike. No one has written odes or glorious songs of his fatherhood, of his manhood, of his awkward and ungraceful fidelity. Until now.

Mary Anne Evans, writing under the pseudonym George Eliot, expressed honorably in the novel, *Middlemarch*, "The growing good of the world is partly dependent on unhistorical acts; and that things are not so ill with you and me as they might have been, is half owing to the number who lived faithfully a hidden life, and rest in unvisited tombs."

I am daring now to be that historian, to be the one who tells the story, cleaving to the coffin in the angry sea like Ishmael, choosing to remember my father differently. I visit his tomb on a nightly basis, journeying in delightful and terror-stricken remembrance alike. For memory is mostly subjective, a choice we get to make while being tossed by the waves of years gone by, seeking the distant shores of home. Of forgiveness. Of a sort of accidental manhood.

The process exists in the liminal, the space in between Toni Morrison's astute observation, between death, the meaning of life and language, the measure of our lives.

I long to be a different kind of man. A different kind of father to my boys. A means of healing for my father. I'm often convinced that through my efforts in fathering differently is how my father may learn, may heal. His father, and the whole ancestral line of Herzog men, may also learn rest and repose, hungry ghosts no longer.

And yet knowing that I am that same kind of man as him. The same DNA. The same blood circulating and recirculating, often diluted with the same amber hues of bourbon. The same marrow that once coursed through his bones with expectation and disappointment. The same husk of bone that bore that marrow, heated, and disintegrated in the fiery bowels of the crematorium into the shards that now rested in my pocket.

Guardian Rock perched resolutely above the campus was the closest thing to a headstone, to a tomb where I might be able to visit my father in the physical realm and pay homage to his hidden life. A life hidden from me. Perhaps even hidden from himself, like so many men of his generation, awash in dreams deferred and responsibilities realized during the banality of post-war promise. It felt right to return the shards and dust of his remains to this place, to the outcropping of volcanic rock blanketed in lichen and moss and flakes of memories of a subterranean life peeking out into the light of day.

This grand rock, holding vigil on the hill above the Institute of Noetic Sciences, lay at the end of a short hike up the hill from the buildings and the labyrinth and sweat lodge and meditation huts, among the other sundry spiritual outcroppings at home in this part of Northern California.

Apollo 14 astronaut Edgar Mitchell founded IONS after he returned from his mission orbiting around the Moon, feeling a sense of oneness while watching the blue ball of Earth rise from his view from the Apollo spaceship.

The sprawling campus sits atop beautiful rolling hills near the town of Petaluma, home to the rich soil and fertile fishing rivers and tributaries from the San Francisco Bay. The Indigenous Miwok tribe lived among these hills, sharing in its dark, volcanic soil and ample fish and game supply. The good Miwok folks have since been replaced by the earnest and yoga-panted crowd from Marin and Sonoma Counties and beyond, searching for spiritual connection with the land amid the bounty of organic kombucha, half-caf oat milk lattes and ample bunches of kale.

IONS participates in remarkable and rigorous research on the connections between spirit and matter, between those things that we can see and those things that we can only sense through the haze of our normal consciousness. Like I stood now, between the matter of the crags and crevices of my father's ashes to his spirit that eluded and called me alike. IONS also hosts a myriad of retreats and rents out space to like-minded partners, like Meridian University where I was beginning my doctoral program in psychology. I had moved my family to the San Francisco North Bay hinterlands, the verdant hub for public-Waldorf education. I had also set my sights on psychology graduate programs in the Bay Area, ranging from the hallowed Stanford and Berkeley campuses to the more avant-garde California Institute of Integral Studies and my fierce, little school, Meridian University. engaged in the work of individual and cultural transformation.

I began the program while my father and our family had just been through the gauntlet of his dying process. I was raw and filled with grief, moving haltingly through my day feeling as if my heart was beating slowly and methodically on the outside of my chest for all the world to see. The rhythms of that heartbeat were at times discordant and disorganized, and occasionally missing a beat. It seemed like an odd, if not formative, time to begin graduate studies in psychology, but I imagined that the program with its intimate cohort model might be able to hold me in my grieving process with tenderness and compassion.

My longing for these sweet and tender feelings was unceremoniously met with a stark bitch-slap from the Universe, a clarion call to wake up and be entirely present to the fullness and pathos of grief and sadness, of longing and suffering. The first book assigned was *The Father*, a cheeky and rumbling Jungian roll through the hijinks of fathering, from the personal to the collective to the archetypal.

I braved my way through the initial classes and discussions on fathers and fathering, maintaining a stone-faced and stone-hearted decorum. I stayed entirely in my head, talking *about* and *around* the grief of losing my father, of his complicated legacy, of the rage and shame that I incurred and also visited upon my children in similar if not diluted ways. Rather than *experiencing* grief. Until I did.

And the psychic floodgates poured open. It was as if I was re-experiencing the full breadth of the experiences of violence, of rage and shame, all over again. My nervous system felt like an old-school pinball game on tilt, lights flashing, bells and whistles pealing and pinging through the echo chambers of my heart and mind. The long-standing grief, hidden in the shadows and corners of my body and soul, was now being unveiled and unbound. This is what I had resisted for years, fearing that I might implode if I ever were to experience the full impact of the grief. My mind had participated in a sort of forgetfulness, at least a presumed forgetfulness, gathering up the necessary strategies and bulwarks against this unyielding tide.

But my body paid a price. Years of football, from age nine through college certainly contributed, but it is no wonder that I experienced a troublesome and sometimes debilitating stress fracture in my lower back dating back to junior high. During this first semester in my graduate school program, it was as if the re-experiencing of the traumas had overwhelmed the scaffolding of my vertebral structure, collapsing into a piercing pain in my neck, my ribs, and my lower back. I felt that I could collapse into an invertebrate puddle, incapable of movement outside of primordial ooze seeping across the floor.

This may all seem abjectly masochistic, as I had signed up and paid handsomely for the privilege of putting myself through this sublime mess. The school believes strongly in the notion of students and fledgling psychologists and therapists going through their own work before ever daring to sit across from someone in a therapy office. It is one thing to participate in an intellectual process of the "how" of doing therapy. It is quite another to descend into the abyss of one's own experience, hopefully coming out on the "other side" transformed, bearing the sacred scars of the process. And understanding the emotional landscape of the descent, having stumbled painstakingly but gloriously through its terrain.

This is not a solo process. Dante had his Virgil, Frodo his Samwise. Don Quixote his Pancho Sanchez, Laverne her Shirley. The hangover from the twentieth-century rave fueled by the soundtrack of Freud and Jung has been the coronation and tyranny of the individual. We laud and venerate the rugged cowboy, Marlboro Man, or Silas Marner-type character, boot-strappin' and smoking unfiltereds all the way through life, a celebration of triumphalism and extolling self-made men and women bearing the spirit of Ayn Rand books. The concept has bored its way into the collective conscious and unconscious of the culture, from the Red Scare and Cold War fighting Communism's bedeviling of our "way of life;" to how we've read/misread Darwin and applied his theories; to how we've read/misread the teachings of Jesus and applied His theories; to how we've done psychotherapy—isolating, diagnosing, and fetishizing the individual ego.

We are compelled to participate in memory, to remember our divinity and our humanity that are bound up with our souls and are our birthright. To remember our ancestors, those who came before us who passed on their DNA, passed on the sins of their mothers and fathers, passed on family lore, passed on their culture and their language, their heartache, and their joys. We bear them all. And just as optimism can be differentiated from hope, memory can be differentiated from mere recall, from simple cascades of neurotransmitters crossing in tight formation across lonely synapses. Memory is complicated and textured, somewhere beyond the pale of mere recall.

Indigenous ancestor-worshipping cultures, Mexican culture, and the rites of remembrance like the soulful Dia de Los Muertos, all have something to teach us in our forward-thinking and futuristic Western take on time, on dying and living. African cultures re-imagine the processes of our lives being lived with an expansive view of the past that lies before us, not behind us, and certainly contrasted with the future-insistent culture of the west—especially of we Americans. Instead, we find ourselves learning and loving through and among all the experiences of our past, while walking ever so slowly and methodically backward into our future.

Time does not simply careen forward; it moves backward toward those who have come before us toward our ancestors in all their vainglory and wonder. As peace monger John Paul Lederach writes in *The Moral Imagination*, "The journey of life moves forward toward physical death, which is a future event. Yet when people die…they join the ancestors in the past. The journey is toward a past that lies before us. The past and future are not seen as dualistic, polar opposites. They are connected, like ends of a circle that meet and become seamless."

This may be the quintessential difference in perspective between Indigenous cultures, immersed in the complexity of memory and ancestors, and western cultures, consumed with controlling the ever-elusive and beguiling future—our fear of succumbing to the force of Death. We bandy about in pursuit of an envisioned Manifest Destiny, looking forward and moving into the Western frontier of possibility, assured that our efforts and machinations will propel us into our long awaited and prolific fates, one step ahead of the ravages and savages of time and our inevitable demise. We are quite adept at forgetting, at divorcing ourselves from our Original Sins, both culturally and personally, damning the torpedoes and moving full steam ahead. We build bridges and we get over it, finding it silly to remember our past, let alone learn from it.

"Fuck your feelings," the angry populist political class shouts.

And yet, there is a force for regaining and resuming a nostalgic way of life, a controlled and hermetically sealed utopian vision when men were kings of their castles, and women, children, dogs and even the culture served at their beck and call. Man as his own sort of city-state, making the rules and enacting the laws, maintaining order, and fortifying walls to protect the subjects from the barbarians lurking at the gate.

It is this paradoxical push and pull with time that makes Western culture so perplexing. We eschew our past, yet still try to control it and return to it, all the while imagining a future in which we are triumphal, vanquishing the forces of anxiety of our impending death through our indomitable will. Czech writer Milan Kundera had a conspicuous view of this iron will behind the Iron Curtain, "The struggle of man against power is memory against forgetting," he writes in *The Book of Laughter and Forgetting*.

We grow in our understanding of the world, of this strange relationship between chaos and order by studying the nature of change. We hoard wealth, experiences, serial monogamous relationships—all bearing a sense of ephemeral—as a means of buttressing us against the anxiety of change.

But change is complicated. Innocence is simple. We long for those simpler times, or at least what we remember as simple. We want our innocence returned and we want it now, damn it. We want to return to the Garden. We want immortality, it seems. Unfortunately, the entrance to the Garden is guarded by angels with flaming swords. Innocence must go through the gauntlet of experience.

Poet Rainer Maria Rilke has a remarkable line about our relationship with the Divine, with all of the humanity that we dare to bear in our deliciously complex and sublime lives, "Take your well-disciplined strengths, stretch them between the two great opposing poles, because inside human beings is where God learns." We hold the spark of the Diving within us, embodied and ensouled, while delighting and commiserating with this great force of God that is still able to learn within ourselves and our myriad of experiences. It is equally riveting and frightening, a *mysterium tremendum* that we boldly remember and wrestle with.

And it is inside us where our parents and ancestors embrace the opportunity for learning as well. This is not solely an intellectual exercise, as we have all no doubt been made to pause and marvel at the sweetness and generational redemption of even the most hardened and toxic parents, as they hold their newborn granddaughter in their arms or teeter across the lawn, hand in hand with their grandson taking his first few steps. They can remember the undeniable and unmitigated goodness, liberated from the genetic imperative of their own rage and grief, of shame and violence visited upon them. And we dare to hope for the same thing for our own children and grandchildren, that they may share in the generational transformation as we learn right along with them and through them.

I carry a picture of my father, one of a few where he is expressive and dare, I say, even happy—an emotion I rarely saw expressed in his day-to-day existence. A furtive glance at work in his overalls, a stylish jacket with his Army buddies in front of the Eiffel Towers, and this one of him holding his grandson, who happens to sport the same hairline as my father's Army issue high and tight buzzcut. It has been said that all babies at one point resemble Winston Churchill. Singer-songwriter John Gorka has a wonderful song in which he croons, "My baby looks like Charles Bronson when he cries."

Similarly, all babies look like my father: wrinkled, missing a neck, furrowed brow beset by random patches of hair hovering just above the fray of forehead wrinkles. Still, my father's eyes appear heavy in the photo, holding the weight of his life spent longing for some other existence, some other circumstance. They are yellowed, those steel blue-colored eyes awash in a sea of jaundice, a sign of the cancer having migrated from his lungs to his liver.

But amazingly and wonderfully they also hold a sparkle, as he beams at this little boy in his arms, my boy in his arms, evoking a memory—imagined or real, I cannot be certain—of him holding me in his arms. There is a genetic imperative for sure, at a deep level he seems content with the knowledge that his genes will carry on for at least another generation. Herzog men persist it seems, even if they don't necessarily flourish. They continue. They show up. They come, they see, they fight, and sometimes they surrender. But they dare to conquer.

They dare to act. The concepts of memory and action are then partnered, one cannot remember without acting. This is consistent with the idea contained in the Hebrew root word, *zkr*. Unlike English, and much like memory itself, Hebrew is textured and nuanced, and a word can take on many meanings depending on the vowels that are added to the root, such as different Hebrew words like *zkar, askarah* or *zikkaron*. At its essence, *zkr* means to remember, of something that rises up to the heart. And the heart partners with the will, fortifying the memory with a sense of action, of stored energy made kinetic, animating the memory, or thought with action. The memory—the event, the emotion, the song that was playing when I kissed Lisa Camp at her sixteenth birthday party, when I received the Call telling me that my father had died—that thing is called forth in the soul and impels the will to act on that call.

A memory, by definition, exists in the past, with remembrance, in the act of *zakar*, that memory transcends time and becomes present and operative in the present moment. This is holy time, time outside of time, described by the Greeks as Kairos. In mythic lore, Chronos is the monster who devours his children. Time has a way of eroding things, of a small, persistent stream smoothing out rocks and pebbles in its gentle wake to the eradication of the cartilage in my knees and other sundry joints that makes me snap, crackle, and pop when I plop down on my couch. One of the beings closest to approximating eternal, persistent beauty, Sophia Loren, insisted that the way to keep from getting old was to refrain from making noises when getting up or sitting down.

Memory can be imbued with past and future—all in a remarkable experience of a remarkable and radical present. It is akin to the Jewish Passover feast: Passover is a confirmation of the presence of God—here and now with His people. Passover is a proclamation of the message of salvation (past); and Passover's intercessory prayer reminds God of His promise (future).

The richness of memory is echoed in the words of Jesus at the Last Supper, celebrated on Sundays throughout the world during Catholic Mass. The priest will hold the consecrated host, the stale wafer or homemade honey wheat bread if you're lucky, transubstantiated into the Body of Christ, the ultimate act of incarnation, of the Logos made flesh. "Do this in memory of me," he bellows to the congregation and into the Void. It is the concept of anamnesis, the idea of remembrance that carries with it a force of will, a call to action contained in the Hebrew *zkr*. Even if that action was ringing the bells on cue, from my perch as an altar boy at St. Susanna's Catholic Church on Stotler Road in Penn Hills. Or sloughing up the center aisle to cannibalize the Body of Christ while the choir hidden behind St. Susanna's 1970s architectural sensibilities rang out earnest and flat hymns and hallelujahs.

The Logos is made flesh, the spirit breathed into physical form into the first Adam and the first Eve. And flesh returns to dust, and in between we live and love, with reckoning and redemption, with hubris and with humility. Our innocence dares to persist through the pathos of experience.

I held a little bit of that dust, my father's measure of that pathos, the various hues of gray ash in the small plastic baggie absconded from that gray metal box I buried in the hard clay over the hill from my boyhood home. I sat cross-legged on the floor of the classroom, of the property on the IONS campus, down the hill from Guardian Rock, where I imagined spreading his ashes in one final ritual, the final act in burying my father.

We have been participating in rites of burial of our dead for thousands of years, from the earnest funeral rites of ancient cave dwellers to embalming our loved one's bodies with various chemicals and shades of blush and lipstick. The various layers of makeup and the impeccable cleaning, ironing, and starching of her favorite dress make our dearly departed Aunt Sallie look presentable in her open casket, inspiring the not so faint praise of "she looked so peaceful" that the makeup inspires during those awkward moments at the wake when we don't quite know what to say to grieving family members as we deal with our own anxieties of inevitable death.

And in this process of ritual, there can exist moments of sweet encounter with the Sacred. The idea of encounter is centered in reciprocity and reflexivity, in that you enter into a sort of dialogue with this moment. You are affected by it, and it is affected by you. African American futurist and prophetess, Octavia Butler, reminds us, "What you touch, you change. What you change, changes you. The only constant is change. God is change."

That change is constant, and yet, there is also a sense of change existing in dialogue with the *unchangeable*. There is a fixed reality within the chaos, a dose of unexpected order in the process of falling apart. The Eternal and timeless enters into a static and precise moment of time—*Kairos* and *Chronos* are married. Something new is born, in a process Jung called the transcendent function. When two forces come together, a new third is created, new life born from the dialogue of two other forces. It is like asking that awkward question of our parents, "Where do babies come from?" "Well, when two people love each other, sometimes they express their love in a physical way..." First comes love, second comes marriage, third comes Bobby in a baby carriage.

I couldn't wait for the lunch break between classes. I had the baggie filled with ashes, a resolute sense of mission and purpose, imagining hurrying up the path to Guardian Rock to spread the ashes in the nooks and crannies of the rock promontory looking protectively over the campus, and about 45 minutes to complete the task and return for my next class.

My father's dying wish had been to be buried with his dogs. I didn't think he would mind a slight detouring of his remaining gray matter to be spread in such a remarkably beautiful resting place. I was in school for the long haul, delightfully immersed in this seven-year project, so I imagined Guardian Rock being a wonderful figurative and quite literal touchstone for my father's presence, being almost 3,000 miles away from my boyhood home in Pittsburgh.

One of the administrative reps sauntered into the classroom space to make a harried announcement, unexpected but certainly not without precedent, "Bring your lunch back into the classroom so we can go over a few things."

My heart dropped. And then my anger seethed. I could certainly have asked to skip the meeting, but my still evolving emotional skillset as a psychologist-to-be had not gotten over my longstanding habit of resentful rule-following.

I don't remember a thing about the meeting, as I concentrated instead on playing with the baggie of ashes, pushing, and pulling the ashes from one end of the bag to the other in a sort of mindless play. This is the last time that I would hold them in my hands.

And that's when I saw it.

I couldn't believe my eyes. There, in one corner of the baggie, was a small, metal circular object. I looked closer, wondering what on earth it could be. As I examined the copper-colored circle more closely, I noticed the small hole in the center on one side. I flipped it over in my fingers observing the tight metal spiral that seemed like some compact, constrained spring.

How had this thing gotten into the baggie of his ashes, I wondered? Could it have been in the bag already, a conveyor belt mishap at the

Ziploc factory? No, it looked too weathered and old to have taken place more recently. Perhaps a piece of metal had inadvertently sprung loose at the crematorium.

Then I remembered.

My father had been in a horrible car accident when I was six years old. A woman had run a stop sign and t-boned right into the driver's side door of my father's green station wagon. He had to be pried out from the wreckage by the Jaws of Life, the damaged side of the car too crumpled to allow the firefighters and EMTs to get access to him any other way. He had broken his hip and his pelvis in multiple places, rendering him helpless and in traction in the hospital for six weeks, back when they still did that.

He endured a painful rehab just to regain the ability to walk. His hip had healed but I don't think his spirit ever did. My father limped through life.

The small, copper-colored circle must have been a piece of hardware, a spring cog in the gears from my father's artificial hip before Titanium proved to be the metal of choice used in evolving joint replacement technology. It had somehow withstood the intensity of the flames and survived the cremation process.

I dropped it suddenly back into the baggie when I realized what it was.

And then I had one of those moments where the eternal crashes in on the temporal, interpenetrating one another in a sublime arrangement. I was clearly paying less attention to the inane school meeting, catapulted into a transition space between Here and There, between the conscious and the unconscious, hanging precariously between Kairos and Chronos.

I remembered. *Zakar*. Something was rising up to my heart. To my mind.

To the memory of a dream that I had the night before, this hip replacement hardware was an unexpected catalyst for my unconscious cascade.

Oscar Wilde quipped, "The most frightening words of the English language are 'I had an interesting dream last night.'" And yet the dream, I maintain, is remarkable. No, really. I swear.

The dream opened in my childhood home with a sense that I needed to find something, someone. I ran to the back deck and jumped over the railing, landing with a thud at the feet of a Zulu warrior in full regalia, an imposing figure over seven or eight feet tall, looming over me like a giant. He pointed silently in the direction of the side of the house.

I scurried over, because, well…you listen to Zulu warriors in your dream.

I came to a small uphill ramp, nestled between the first floor of the house and the basement. A long concrete ramp with a strange figure at the end of the shadowy space. There, without much panic or fanfare, at least from him, was a five-year old boy, five-year old me, wrapped in the copper coils of an enormous snake. The snake was the same color and had the same tight, compact coils as the spring that I had found at the bottom of the baggie of my father's ashes.

The piece of hardware that made me remember this dream.

I panicked, afraid that the boy was being attacked. As I looked more closely, I saw that the snake was wrapped around the boy in protection. The boy showed no dismay, no panic, no pain at being held tightly but safely within the coiled power of the serpent. At any moment, just one small exertion of constriction could crush the boy, like a poor unsuspecting rodent held in the tight grasp of a boa constrictor on those Mutual of Omaha programs with Marlon Perkins.

The Zulu warrior spoke in a gravely, baritone voice filled with gravitas, "It is time for the boy's rite of passage."

In my waking consciousness, I had studied other cultures and their rites of passage often prescribed for boys at the cusp of adolescence—at thirteen or fourteen years old. I had even worked at an organization that conducted rites of passage for men of all ages, as a means of remembering and restoring the long-forgotten cultural responsibility of marking the crossing of threshold from boy to man.

What my father had longed for and never received.

I knew the boy in the dream, me, even my father; we were all too young.

"He's not ready!" I implored.

"It does not matter," the Zulu warrior responded sternly but lovingly.

And then the recollection of the dream was over. And the meeting was over. My heart pounded resoundingly in my chest. I could hear the staccato rhythm of the blood pulsing in my eardrums. I would not be attending that afternoon's class.

I took the baggie of ashes and marched with purpose up the trail to Guardian Rock. Upon arrival at the end of the short trail, I marveled at the mid-afternoon sun illuminating grays and whites and speckles of geological alchemy shining from the shards and angles of this piece of Sierran granite that looked over the green hills of the IONS campus. I spread the various shards and angles of my father's bones at the base of the rock, sprinkling bits of the powder in the crevices and platforms created by wind, moisture, time, and pressure. A gentle, unexpected breeze picked up and scattered the more powdery parts of the ashes down the hill.

I fiddled with the copper spring in my pocket. That I was going to keep to myself.

I have since graduated from that school with my PhD in psychology. I work with different clients, including fathers and sons. Of all ages. Mothers and daughters. too. But the boys, the men—they have a special place in my clinical world and in my heart. Some of them tell wonderful stories of their fathers in their grief—of fishing trips and baseball games and the smell of his aftershave or his study. Others tell me horrifying tales of toxic fathers, of abuse and rage, of violence and betrayal. They speak of sins of commission, sins of omission, of staying when they shouldn't have and abandoning them when they should have stayed.

They remember. And I remember with them.

My school moved its campus into town a few years into my long slog of doctoral studies. It's not as dramatic or quite as beautiful as the sprawling campus in the hills just over the border of Marin County. I would still visit Guardian Rock on special days like my dad's birthday or on the anniversary of his death.

A sort of pilgrimage.

I bring supplies for the journey, of course. A cigar to smoke in his memory. A good cigar, not those nasty Winchester little things he liked to chain smoke neurotically. I tell him he deserves a better quality of cigar. I stick with his whiskey of choice though, stopping at the liquor store to buy an airplane-sized bottle of Jack Daniels. I take a small swig and pour the rest of it out for him.

I make sure I take off my hiking boots when I get up there. It's holy ground, a place to be literally grounded in memory of the ancestors. Like when Yahweh commanded Moses to remove his sandals on Mt. Sinai. I don't know if the one true God ever commanded his good and faithful servant to remove his robe, but for a while there I would sit there at the rock naked. No secrets. No barriers.

At least until my visit was interrupted one time by a nice couple of gray-haired women taking a break from whatever workshop they were attending at IONS to make their own pilgrimage to Guardian Rock. They helped me to have more barriers, putting some of my clothes back on, appropriate to public spaces.

My father and I would talk with our clothes on after that. I told him stories about his grandsons and all of their exploits. I could imagine him laughing with delight. I even brought my boys up there once before IONS got more serious about keeping visitors off their campus. They didn't have cigars, but they may have taken a sip or two from the small whiskey bottle well before their twenty-first birthdays.

On one of those visits there was a beautiful black crow spreading its wings, playing in the wind drafts in the canyon overlooking the school. My oldest son, Silas, remarked, "That must be Pop Herk's spirit up there."

All four of us sat quietly and enjoyed the prospect of that boy's wise thought.

I wear that copper-colored circle, that strange talisman I found at the bottom of his ashes, around my neck sometimes, having commissioned an artist to make it into a necklace.

I remember him. I remember him differently at different times.

And he remembers me. We are bound together. And I am bound to my boys.

I hope that they remember me too.

Chapter Ten

To foster a unified humankind, we must do away with the enmity and struggles that divide humans, and the living sons must join together for the resurrection of their dead fathers.

N.F. Fyodorov

Like most men of a certain generation, I had not seen my father cry often. I had seen the glassy and bloodshot eyes of a drunkard staring back at me. I had seen him stubbornly teary-eyed when one of the family dogs died, and he would have to bury them in the backyard. Depending on how many beers he had consumed. I swear he would shed a tear or two of joy when his beloved Steelers hoisted another Super Bowl trophy.

But the full breakdown sob, shoulders heaving, grief-released kind of cry? Not my father's inclination.

My boys have seen me cry. Multiple times. I'm a sucker for sad movies, celluloid sentimentality, and even occasional moments of real-life grace and grief. And there is always a moment of pause for me, as old stories, and my father's gruff voice echo in my mind, "Stop crying, or I'll give you something to cry about."

My mother let me know that I had made my father cry the night of our confrontation on the back porch of my childhood home, a few feet from where I would eventually bury him. She told me that he had sobbed uncontrollably, his body shaking, snot and spit spewing from ancient reservoirs of grief and shame.

She would not forgive me this unpardonable sin, the blaspheming of her Holy Spirit, the man who had saved her from her own fatherless void. For making my father break open as he stared down the inevitability of his hastening death. She blamed me for his dying. Or at least for the suffering she imagined that I caused him.

I'm not sure I have entirely forgiven myself. I certainly regret what I said, or at least how I said it. He died before I could take it all back, or reframe it, or even apologize I suppose. As Kevin Costner's character, Ray Kinsella, laments in *Field of Dreams*, "The son of a bitch died before I could take it back." My mother cast me out into family exile, bearing all of the family sins, a scapegoat cast out to be ground into the dust of a lonely, arid orphan desert.

I made my way back to Pittsburgh through the fog of memory and the deeper fog of my father's cancer prognosis. It turned out to be the last time that I would see him. His eyes were tinged with deep hues of jaundiced yellow, the cancer having spread from his lungs to his spine to his liver. To him, nothing had changed. He still smoked a pack or two of his Winchester Little Cigars every day. He still occupied that same seat in the kitchen in front of the TV, with that same glass of Penn Hills legendary Turner's Iced Tea, although he had transitioned to the unsweetened version because of his diabetes. He still had a twelve pack of Iron City Light in the refrigerator, the light beer a concession he had made to his long-time family doctor.

I remember having watched an educational video in grade school about the ills of smoking, even getting to handle a cancer-addled lung with its black-tarred surface. I had already sworn off smoking, having to endure my clothes bearing the embarrassing fetid odor of cigarettes as I sheepishly wandered the halls of Dible Elementary hoping not to be noticed. I changed into my clothes every day before school in the cold concrete confines of the garage—the furthest indoor point away from my parents' two-pack-a-day habit. Yet the smell persisted.

I calculated how much money the family would save if they quit smoking. I shoved small exploding seeds into the front of their cigarettes, creating a startling bang when the ash heated up after a few puffs. I even threw out cartons of cigarettes in the trash as my first act of civil disobedience, having to retrieve them from the layers of coffee grounds, eggshells, and cigarette butts after they beat my ass for the indiscretion. But they both kept smoking. They smoked more in response to my earnest attempts at a smoking cessation intervention.

"You gotta' die of something, Bobby," he would insist when I asked him why he would not ever stop smoking.

And now he was.

Dying.

Of something. Of cancer.

I wondered if he was grateful to be dying. He never seemed to delight much in being alive. For so long, he lived like the Fisher King, Anfortas—literally "him without power"—in the story of Parsifal and the search for the Holy Grail. Anfortas was neither able to fully live nor succeed in the ultimate attempt at dying. That scared me, shook me to the bone. Was this to be my legacy? To bear this sadness and sense of tragedy that occupied and eventually smothered the men in my family. Would my sons bear that same sense of dread and melancholy? I could begin to see it in them. I had always recognized it in myself. Fought it. Raged against at times.

I had also learned that rage, the unholy anger that seems supremely and tragically accessible to most men. Anger serves as a means of expression of grief and shame that cannot find healthy outlets. Anger as the inevitable eruption of unfelt, untended, and silent suffering. As James Baldwin insists, "I imagine one of the reasons people cling to their hate so stubbornly is because, once hate is gone, they will be forced to deal with pain."

I had come home in an attempt to understand my father's version of the family sadness, insistent on believing that the encounter with his inevitable decline might allow for insights to be shared, or at least for unspoken family narratives to be finally expressed. I needed to know. I needed to avoid the same fate. I needed to spare my boys from this suffering that seemed almost inevitable as heirs to the Herzog patrilineal dis-ease. But my father resisted, consistently, remaining de-animated and oblivious to this time of transition, this time of dying. He was dying like he lived. Most of us do, I suppose.

He would occasionally change the venue for his smoking and alternating iced tea and beer swilling. He and my mother would assume their positions on the back deck off the kitchen, the perch their pride and joy overlooking the glade of trees just beyond the postage stamp backyard, sharing an ashtray on the small table between them and watching the family dog find just the right tree to pee on. The trees where my father would be buried in a few months.

I laid on the chaise lounge, my legs stretched out, hands clasped behind my head—attempting to look casual while my sense of mission as family investigative reporter made my anxiety levels soar. My mouth was dry, my stomach flipped and flopped in anticipation of asking the right question. I was not sure what that question might sound like, even though I had rehearsed it multiple times on the drive to Pittsburgh. On my drive home.

I stammered through the first attempt. "Dad, I would sure like to talk with you."

"Well, I'm right here. What the hell do you wanna' talk about?"

My mother squirmed in her seat, lighting up another cigarette.

"I have so many questions for you, Pops. I'm not sure where to start."

He looked at me with a sideways glance that used to stop me in my tracks when I was a kid. I thought about remaining silent or worse yet, participating in our usual banal banter about the weather, or the Steelers, or my job. Nonetheless, I persisted.

"This may be the last time we talk, Pops."

"Geezus, what do you mean?"

"You have cancer, Dad. You're dying." I could feel the bile rise in my throat, my mouth getting even drier, as my heart and mind swirled in a furor of emotions—sadness, anger, shame, the Unholy Trinity of feelings that gripped the men of my family—and most men.

"I don't have cancer. *I have a condition.*"

There it was. It all made sense in the midst of its nonsense. My father was indeed dying as he had lived, stilted and awash in oblivion, unaware or at least unwilling to experience his full Experience. Or at least what I imagined he should be experiencing. This kind of thinking was focused on myself, imagining that I might be healed if he would only become more aware and enlightened in his dying process. I longed for an awareness of dying that he could not conjure in his waking life. I longed for his blessing. Surely, he might grant me that elusive blessing, his desperation for wanting to make things right matching my own desperation for healing.

I could not imagine that he might very well be despairing, gripped by the prospect of a life unlived and a death that was approaching with an exponential acceleration. An acceleration into a void, an unknowing that he could not abide. But I demanded that he abide. That he might be sacrificed for my own well-being.

Sacrifice. It is what men do. They sacrifice themselves for God and country, for an ideal, something bigger than themselves. Even for their sons.

This was yet another betrayal by my father that I could construct to assuage my own suffering. He resisted the noble sacrifice. He could not dare to step up and exercise what I imagined fathers were supposed to do, supposed to be. What I needed him to be in my aggrieved fantasy. I could not concede to his letting go. He had let go, abdicated any sense of identity and fortitude a long while ago, sliding into a de-animation of sorts, a benign forgetfulness between being and non-being.

I was angry with him, resentful that he could not be what I needed him to be. Not tending to who he was, merely grieving what he wasn't and what he could not be. I reached for him, across the Void, across the gap that existed between us in our own lives as father and son, and in the lives of fathers and sons of our ancestors. I longed for connection, a transmission of his blessing, of his power. Before he slipped into full forgetfulness. Before I forgot him.

To be oblivious is to exist in a state of forgetting. To forget is to be estranged, set apart, alienated, even exiled. In Latin, to be estranged means "not belonging to the family." My father had never felt like he belonged, like so many men of his generation. Like so many sons of my generation. Like me. We all long to belong. I even imagine that my father shared this natural longing, although he lacked the vocabulary to articulate it. To long is to acknowledge suffering, to entertain the paradox between the truth that we are whole and belong to a beloved Community of Being while living in a culture that sells the lie—and sells it well—that we are separate, isolated, and alienated. We as men on the cusp of Elderhood must name and tend to our brothers, sons, and fathers in the gap between longing and belonging.

In her wonderful book, *The Power of Gentleness: Meditations on the Risk of Living*, Anne Dufourmantelle states, "When we are seized by the feeling that nobody will ever come to us, ever, we must still find the strength to extend our arms, to kiss, to love. To say it, to start again, to hear the whisper of that wild voice that calls you from well before your beginnings."

I could not share the antidote, the kiss, the love, the whisper held in asking the right question. I had not journeyed long enough to have my anger and resentment transformed by the compassion that is born from the sublime experience of ten thousand joys and ten thousand sorrows. I was in my own state of exile, convinced that I was alone and oblivious. I was reaching across the gap between father and son, the gap between fathers and sons of my own ancestors, and the gap that has existed between fathers and sons throughout time. The terror experienced by Jesus as he was hanged on a cross, his punishment and sacrifice for challenging the patriarchy of his time and imagining a different way of being—"My God, my God, why hast thou forsaken me?"

And then I snapped.

I cajoled. I implored. I sobbed. I raged.

I spoke the most hurtful things I could have imagined. I challenged his identity as a man and a father.

"You never showed me anything! You never taught me anything! You left me!"

I was speaking to my father. While I raged at God, at the Universe, at the cruelty of uncaring and punishing Fates. My father was but a proxy for those inevitable forces. He, tragically, did not understand the difference. Nor did I at the time, even more tragically.

I was not thinking, my mind and brain swirling in emotional furor. Somewhere I imagined that this level of verbal violence might push him toward revelation, toward epiphany, toward extending his blessing to me.

I acted like Judas in his well-documented and unsubtle misinterpretation of *his* betrayal, who identified Jesus with a kiss on the cheek as the thirty pieces of silver jingled in the pocket of his robe. Judas meant to push the situation, to push Jesus into the inevitability of morphing from gentle, wise teacher and prophet to conquering Savior, rallying righteous and destructive angelic forces to defeat the occupying Roman forces.

After I had finished my tirade with neither fatherly epiphany nor conquering angels, my parents remained awkwardly silent, squirming in their deck lounge chairs on squeaky, sweaty cushions. My shoulders heaved, and the feeling returned to my fingers and toes, the tingling of restored blood flow coursing through my veins. My body had mustered the troops, galvanizing all of my energies into a protean evolutionary rage, diverting life force into this one last battle for survival. My father was dying. And I had to survive, with or without his blessing. I would have to go on without it, bearing the wound that most sons carry into their extended adolescence, longing to be men.

He was right. He did not only have cancer, but he also had a condition. His was a condition shared by most men in silent, aggrieved complicity. He had not received the blessing from his own father, missing his birthright, even though he shared the veneer of his father's name. He had been conditioned to withhold the blessing from his son. Sins of the fathers, and their fathers, visited on sons. He had not crossed the threshold into manhood, like his own father, and I imagine, his father before him. I could not bear to imagine doing that to my own sons.

Can't you see, father, that I am different from you?

Can't you see, Son, that you are your Father's Son, heir to all of the curses of stilted masculinity?

And the blessings.

A deep knowing of the blessings, if nothing else, in their conspicuous absence. To remember the blessings of the Father that were present but not overt, that came in ways unknown to the angry, aggrieved *puer aeternus*, the eternal adolescent.

Blessings that were revealed in my father's stubborn and ungraceful showing up, his presence an unspoken validation. The hours spent huddled in the cold at all of those practices in the unforgiving Pittsburgh winters. The time on the road between the staid enclave of working-class suburbs and the evolving liberal arts horizons of my college. And back again. To secretly grab the sports pages from college newspapers to be collected and glued into the pages of a scrapbook, the holy, yellowing writ of this sacred book carried by me in various cardboard boxes from various moves from place to place in search of an elusive, accidental manhood.

I wished I could have asked him the right questions in that moment of swirling emotions. Like Parsifal in the search for the Holy Grail—who forgets to ask Anfortas, the Fisher King, "What ails you?" The question that most men hardly ever hear.

"How are you?"

And resisting simple answers, "No, really, how are you?"

"I need to know."

For you. For me.

Most men are bound by a sense of duty and sacrifice, noble pursuits for sure, reified by archetypal warrior and provider energies galvanized throughout time. But it can also be a source of denial, shame, and alienation when the inevitable vagaries of life—failed marriages, estranged relationships with distant children, corporate banality—pierce the thick armor of our protective layers.

In the story of the Grail, Parsifal, the young, burgeoning warrior-knight, courses through his journey of fierce becoming. He meets women and stumbles through an encounter with the force of eros, skirmishes with other knights bent on his destruction, and even spends a fateful night at the castle where the hallowed Grail itself resides. The Grail holds the source of his healing, the profundity of which is lost on him in the oblivious denials of youthful hubris and attention to the whims of his growing appetites. It also holds the healing for the Kingdom, which has lain destitute, arid, and lifeless since the King had been wounded in the loins, the source of his life-giving power. The young man's healing and his community's healing are bound together in a radical interdependence. His journey is bound to this revelation. This is the power of the Grail.

Yet Parsifal is repeatedly frustrated in his pursuits, awash in his own oblivion, looking for love in all the wrong places along the way. He has an opportunity to lay bare his soul, to ask the King, "What ails you?" To tend to the King's soul and to the *anima mundi*, the soul of the world, the soul of the Kingdom. The Grail Castle and the holy treasure of the Grail disappear from the young hero, Parsifal, and he is left confused and disappointed. The Kingdom remains unhealed, like the Fisher King wounded in his loin , like so many older men and the unfortunate sons of our generation, the creative and life-giving force pierced by poisoned arrows of grief, shame, and anger.

I may not have known him any better if I had indeed asked the right question. This is the advantage of retrospect and magical thinking, I suppose—to imagine that things would have been radically different if I had just done the Right Thing; asked the Right Question. This is the seduction of the performance model that is reified in most men, the rugged individualist who is solely responsible for his actions and fates, relationship and reality be damned.

There is a danger in imagining clean and unfettered happy endings, neat and tidy narrative arcs that shout at us from television and film narratives and the veneer of social media influencers bent on sharing the opaque, dream-like quality of their perfect lives. Reality is always much messier, the innocence of glorious fantasies compelled to pass through the gauntlet of experience.

None of that dared register with me. None of that could temper my desperation, what I perceived to be my suffering at the hands and fists of my father. I spent a restless night, tossing and turning in the twin bed of my childhood bedroom, the corrugated, slanted walls painted the same light blue of my youth. I could still make out the small indentation in the wall from me practicing my Willie Stargell-inspired home run baseball swing that I covered up with a Steelers poster to hide my sin of aluminum bat commission and avoid the inevitable punishment.

I woke up anticipating the opportunity to continue the discussion, without the same volume or vitriol but working toward a semblance of apology and forgiveness. I still expected my father to extend his long-term apology while I made amends for my more recent transgression. But there would be none of either.

We ate a makeshift breakfast in an awkward silence. My parents swilled their coffee in enormous cups adorned with pictures of Mickey and Minnie Mouse from their most recent trip to Disneyland, the voyage an homage to attempts at finding the Happiest Place in the World. I sat silent, harkening back to thousands of family meals in the small, yellow kitchen—as the television at the center of the table blared with stories from the local news. I was embarrassed for what I had said the previous night, as I imagine my father was as well—shame being an easily accessible emotion meant for us and the other men of my ancestral line.

The Fisher King's wound would persist, unable to be healed in yet another moment of my inability to ask the right question. And my father could not access the power of the Grail, unable to open himself to the possibility of healing in his unflinching and unwavering stubbornness constructed and reified through his years and through generations of wounded men. Like Parsifal, I had woken to find the castle abandoned, access to the Grail denied again, and the Kingdom would remain in squalor, where nothing could grow, its subjects unable to flourish.

I packed my suitcase for the flight back to Albuquerque in a liminal space between grief and resolve, my clothes bearing the familiar smell of cigarette smoke. I could only imagine the smell greeting me like a brick wall of memory upon my return home when I unpacked amid the soft, forgiving confines of my new family home.

My father's eyes were even more yellow and bloodshot, though I barely noticed as he avoided making eye contact with me, both of us stewing in our unspoken embarrassment. My mother seethed in silence as she, too, could barely look at me, angry at me for the suffering I had caused him. I imagined later that the crying I had evoked with my tantrum was a necessary opening for my father, a small crack in the cistern that held years of grief that he dared not feel in his waking consciousness. It was all too much. For both of us. It was simply to assuage the guilt that I felt for making him cry, but I felt resolve, a sublime complicity in participating in pushing him to feel *something*.

And still nothing had changed between us.

We sidled up against each other as in our usual awkward goodbyes, unable to hug yet insistent on sharing a cordial farewell exchange. He reached across time and space and the awkwardness to pat me on my shoulder in an attempt at affection.

"Have a good trip home, Bobby," he stammered.

Home.

The word hit me squarely in the chest, between competing emotions of sadness for not having asked the right question and the desperate gratitude of returning to my own home. To my own family and to my sons who I vowed would receive their blessings without having to wonder or long for their bestowing. How could I allow my own hardened cistern of complicated emotions to crack open, to allow them access to their own healing? That I might learn from them as I longed for my father to be able to learn from me. That the Kingdom might be brought back to life, as the Parsifal story ends, in a state "…of riches without limit, of vigor without cease, of wisdom without end, and of unbroken love between all of humanity."

I tossed my suitcase in the trunk of the rental car, waved goodbye to my mother at the dining room window as she shut the curtains with a begrudging wave of her own, a portend of my family exile. My father was nowhere to be found.

I steered the car toward the airport and the next leg of the journey. This one was ending, reluctantly, but ending, nonetheless. I dared not look back as the car left the driveway down the steep embankment of Clay Drive, knowing in some deep place of my unconscious that I would soon be back at the other end of that driveway, his ashes in my hands.

Chapter Eleven

Never give a sword to a man who can't dance.
Confucius

I'm not sure anyone would confuse my father with Fred Astaire, but he certainly enjoyed dancing. I'm not sure "dancing" is the most accurate word, it was more of an unveiling, a working-class version of Salome and the Dance of the Seven Veils. And like the well-heeled narrative of older white men throughout time, he usually required several beers to get him out on the dance floor.

Family weddings were usually held in the Social Hall above Penn Number 7 Fire Hall, a sort of hallowed Upper Room, antechamber of suburban bacchanal, where Iron City and Budweiser flowed like water from a spring and famous Pittsburgh Italian-American cookie table fed the masses. The cookie table transcended its Italian roots and allowed room for whatever ethnicity—Mick, Polack, Dago—all were welcome to share the bounty of pizzelles, biscotti, and other various bedazzled and iced carbohydrate gems. Aluminum tins of baked ziti, meatballs, and kielbasa warmed under the carefully tended flames of Steno cans.

The men would gather at the bar, elbows leaning on the counter in casual repose as their other elbows bent and re-bent, bringing small cups of beer to their mouths. Many, many small cups of beer. The women, mothers, sisters, aunts, and grandmothers, would congregate as a fortified gaggle on the other side of the hall, giggling over their half-drunk whisky sours and glasses of rose with requisite ice cubes. They would fuss and fawn over the sequined bride, cluck their tongues at their husbands, sons, and fathers who would be plying the groom with shots of Jack Daniels, cajoling him past the threshold of manhood and the life sentence that marriage carried with it, according to their well-practiced "ball and chain" narratives.

The DJ was usually someone's little cousin, whose burgeoning hip-hop scratching career could be put on hold for a brief time to play Kool and the Gang's "Celebration" wedding reception anthem for the sentimentalized masses. The women would invariably be the first on the dance floor, relieved to shed their uncomfortable and rarely worn heels that rubbed up against angry and stubborn bunions. And the fathers would watch from their beer-infused perch, liquid courage coursing through their veins and reviving dusty memories of their own wedding nights. They even imagined that they could get lucky later that night. The only other reason to dance. Whisky dicks and passed out stupors usually had something to say about that.

Something remarkable would happen then. The scantily populated dance floor would suddenly be teeming with couples shaking their groove "thangs," reminiscent of an awkward love shared over years of their disgruntled marriages, divorce a rare option in these hallowed Catholic enclaves. The fights and mutterings and tension over finances would fade away under the glow of strobe lights and the deep bass of stadium rock power ballads. The DJ, with his keen powers of observation, would break into the next phase of his inevitable play list—the Chicken Dance, the Tarantella, and the requisite disco songs that would elevate the energy of the room into some thumping, pulsing expression of pure joy, the laughter pealing over the pounding beat of the Bee Gee's and Commodores. Collective soul at the height of celebration and release—what rites of passage are intended to do for communities.

My father would grow increasingly comfortable with his big-bellied body as he swilled more of those small plastic cups. He had his one infamous move that would be equally hilarious and cringe-worthy for his son—his pants would eventually slide down, a casualty of the war between his protruding gut and his flat old man-ass. He would stop, lower his pants to his ankles, pull up his tent-like boxers over his gut and re-fasten his belt one or two more holes tighter. Then he would grow more comfortable with my mother's body, casually dropping his hand on her ass or grabbing a handful of her boob if his buddies were watching.

And my dad would start sweating. His high and tight crew cut would quickly glisten with the labor of his dancing. He would begin his cruelly slow striptease, progressively removing a layer of dress for relief from the heat until he would strip down to his sleeveless t-shirt, unbuckled pants, and his tie wrapped around his head as a makeshift, silken sweat band. He would forget the pain in his body—the arthritis in his lower back, the mangled big toes and other joints of his feet ravaged by years spent on hard cement factory floors, the hip replacement that could now cut a rug and dance a jig.

He would forget the pain of his soul—the misery of mundane conveyor belts that carried sundry plastic widgets to be machined and packed away in an endless stream, the disappearance of his well-paying nuclear missile tech gig that went the way of détente and perestroika with the ending of the Cold War. He dared to forget in a haze of alcohol and shared smokes with the other neighbor dads, Dick DeFazio, Mike Maguire, and Fred Phillips, all of them sharing in the tension between the prevailing despair and that night's delight, my mother's head resting on his shoulder for a brief moment of ease.

I dreaded what I knew was coming at the end of the night. I was a squirrelly, observant kid, shy, quiet, and relegated to raising my finger in the air to gauge which way the emotional winds might be blowing at any particular moment. These joyous occasions would hit an inevitable peak, and the descent would be quick and unforgiving. My mother would shame my father for drinking too much; my father would shame my mother for "busting his balls" about having a good time, with slurred words and stumbling down the steps to the darkened asphalt parking lot behind the fire hall. My mother would wrest the keys from him, even though he insisted that he could maneuver the trusty family Chevette the mile-and-a-half to our family home.

"Goddamit, I'll just walk," he would scream to my mother. The other families were coursing through their own dramas with their drunken fathers in cars dotted through the parking lot.

My father would think better of walking home and stuff himself into the back seat, resting his head out the open window to feel the cool, summer breeze and convenient access to open space if he had to throw up. I occupied the front seat next to my mother who huffed and shook her head at another night of my father's drunken exploits. He would pass out quickly as we drove down Universal Road toward our house. When I was younger, I often thought that he had died in the back seat, eventually comforted by the snoring and drunken grunts that assured me that he was still alive.

"Aren't we gonna' get Dad out of the car?" I would plead with my mother as we pulled into the driveway.

"Let the son of a bitch sleep in the car!" she insisted.

I wouldn't sleep much on those nights, slipping from my bed in the quiet night to check on my dad. I would gently and then more aggressively shake him by the shoulder to try and wake him up. He usually resisted, grumbling to leave him alone as I laid the sport coat over his back and shoulders to keep him warm in the cool of the summer early morning. And then everything would return to normal in the morning. He and my mother would be sipping their coffee in silence on the back porch, resuming the banality of their utilitarian relationship, as my dad swallowed fistfuls of aspirin with his coffee. This return to normal was confusing for me, wondering how they could act as if the previous night's hijinks had never happened, although I was relieved that the drama might be over for at least one more day. I suppose we all got used to the passion play.

There was one exception to this normal drama and our family's acceptance of it, I discovered much later as I grew accustomed to in my early adult life, as stories and secrets filtered out after my father's death—the statute of limitations having expired. My half-brother recounted to me that one particularly heinous night of wedding reception drinking had inspired my father to stumble from the driveway to his bedroom to retrieve the pistol that he kept in the dark-wooded headboard, insisting against my mother's best judgment that he needed it for "protection."

I imagine that I was sent to my room to avoid seeing the fullness of the spectacle. I have no memory of this happening, but it makes perfect sense in an imperfect way. My father was waving the gun around, threatening to kill himself, vowing to my mother in , "You'll see when I'm gone!" My mother shrieked, my half-brother Chuck and half-sister Barb cowered, although they might have been glad if he had pulled the trigger, having had to endure the violence and hatred of this man who was their stepfather. Even my mother harbored a secret desire for him to pull the trigger, to finally be done with his drama, to be able to rest. I'm sure the desperation of imagined consequences got the better of this thought as she wrestled the gun away from my father, the two of them plopping to the ground as my father wailed and sobbed in her arms, according to my older siblings' report.

Guns were everywhere, the 30 .06 rifles and shotguns adorning the chipped light blue paint of the cinderblock wall that passed for a finished basement. I knew that my father had a handgun somewhere in his bedroom since he and my mother fought about it constantly, the impending threat it posed to the curiosity of a young boy in her anxious estimation. My father had been in the Army and the National Guard for close to thirty years. Each month he would squeeze into his Army fatigues and well-polished combat boots to "play Army" somewhere, my imagination filling in the gaps of his icy quiet as he arrived back home Sunday night griping about having to work seven days in a row.

During summers he would travel to exotic places like Fort Indiantown Gap to blow shit up with his artillery company. My father was immensely proud of having been featured in a Parade Magazine article, brimming with hubris at the photo that showed up in the Sunday papers of homes throughout Pittsburgh and beyond, until it was thrown out with all of the other ads and circulars that people tossed quickly and casually into the trash. He kept a yellowed copy of that picture in his wallet, his own version of the Kilroy Was Here ethos, screaming to the world in jaundiced frayed edges that he had been here and that he had mattered. He kept us safe, ironically, with artillery rounds, Hercules missiles, and all his sundry guns.

Safe.

None of us really felt safe in his presence. His quiet, checked out visage merely existed as a thin layer of veiled protection over the fire that burned hot just under its surface. I'm not sure that he felt particularly safe from the forces that ravaged his perceived bastion of white male power. He needed protection from the corporate forces at work, from the minorities who were moving closer and closer to his neighborhood security and makeshift social apartheid, from the impending and precipitous decline of his body with all its various artificial joints and debilitating arthritis.

The guns may have given him a sense of safety, formidable in his mind but so irretrievably brittle. He was one of the "deplorables" that Hillary Clinton so blithely mentioned, and one of the many referenced by Obama who clung to "religion and guns." Praise Jesus and pass the ammunition.

I resisted his glorification of all things military because that's what sons do. They stake out their own positions, most often in vainglorious opposition to their fathers. I became a pacifist, I cried easily, I needed to be toughened up under the tutelage of various football coaches, part of the same deplorable caste, who would exorcise their own demons of shame on such unsuspecting sinewy lads with oversized shoulder pads and Riddell helmets.

He was amused when I joined the Navy to pay for graduate school, having been abjectly disappointed when I turned down a potential appointment to West Point as a high school senior. He took an enthusiastic satisfaction in my stories of getting "mashed" as punishment by sadistic company commanders at boot camp in Great Lakes, Illinois—performing push-ups and burpees and "cockroach" drills with our arms and legs held up in the air until someone vomited or our spirits were deemed sufficiently broken. These were his people. He hoped that they might make me one of his people. It didn't take.

The Navy is not the Marines or the Army. A little tougher than the Air Force, but certainly debatable. We didn't have to march with M-16's or learn hand to hand combat. There was one opportunity to shoot at things, the seductive power of holding and firing a weapon of such destruction making my boot camp-cohort froth at the mouth with anticipation. The company commanders of our unit were compelled to read the ridiculous-to-them statement from the Department of Defense that once could opt out of small arms training. Everyone around me chuckled at the notion. My hand slowly went up in the back of the formation, my refusal fueling the separation from my father that I longed for, even as I felt at home in this military world, boot camp a breeze compared to the intensity of my father's own version of discipline and violence. From that moment on, I was the "Rev" in my unit, the nickname a combination of ridicule and odd respect.

I was sufficiently uncomfortable then, when my mother placed my father's Beretta 9 mm handgun in the palm of my hand. She wanted to get rid of it but wouldn't dare touch it for too long, as if it might burn her or at least go off in her hand as she imagined. Or she remembered the risk of it going off in my father's hand, whether accidentally or as an autonomous act from his desperation.

"We can sell it. I need the money, Bobby. Your dad's military pension just isn't enough." Her practicality easily drained the small reservoir of sentimentality that she carried. We needed to sell the gun because the military in its eternal wisdom and glee for all things ballistic refused to sufficiently pay back its soldiers who carried those same guns. Carried them in wartime and carried them in peace, fingers precariously hovering over the triggers during both.

I found Powell Guns quite easily. There were a remarkable number of gun shops in the Pittsburgh area, a fact that should not have so easily surprised me, given the area's creature comforts of hunting, self-protection, and anxiety over evolving social trends. Born out of a sense of scarcity that haunted most men—of not enough to eat, not enough to provide for his family, of not enough power, embracing narratives that "Jews would replace him" or "the 'blacks' were coming for his jobs and his women."

The gun shop was an indiscriminate storefront on Frankstown Road in the heart of Penn Hills, just down the street from the municipal building and nestled between a package store and a hair salon. The business had expanded from William Powell's garage to this innocuous store front over 30 years. Mr. Powell had made his money mostly from selling hunting rifles to weekend warriors traipsing through the woods and various handguns to anxious men to protect their families. Business was good and getting better, expanding to long guns and semi-automatic weapons that had tragically become part of the national conversation with the increase in mass shootings.

I must confess that I felt an odd sense of power with the gun in my hand, waiting with my mother in the car outside Powell's, the clip removed and the safety on in unintentional redundancy to prevent the gun from going off accidentally. Or from me pulling the trigger with a sort of mindless deliberateness. I felt the enormity of its weight, of the times that my father drunkenly held it loaded and waving near his head in the midst of another bout of despair. Of the times he may have threatened my mother. Of the times he held the gun in his lap like I was doing now, he perched between consideration of life and death.

As the energy that has held family secrets begins to dissipate, more of our history has been unveiled. Perhaps the narrative of my family is being recapitulated in other interpersonal levels and also in wider cultural narratives as facile trust in institutions wavers. My father's drunken dalliances with handguns had not been his only thoughts of suicide. He had been found at work in his car, in the early predawn hours after the night shift at his factory, Mine Safety Appliances in Murrysville, with the car running. The details remain murky as the density of family secrets resists revelation.

But there was enough concern for the company to mandate my father to see a therapist, worried that he was contemplating suicide. Imagining my father in a therapist's office is intriguing. I have imagined my father on my own therapist's couch or chair; I have certainly played that scenario out in my mind, getting to ask him the "standard" therapy questions, to understand him just a little more, to understand his anger and his shame.

Even to save him. And redeem my own experience as a kid all at the same time. It is no particular secret that many therapists enter into the field as a means of figuring out their own traumas and developmental narratives. Along the way, hopefully, they learn to tease out their own processes from those of their clients. I'm still working on it, as my own history and responses to that history remain constant companions in the room when seeing clients.

What would I ask my father? How would I suggest helping him, healing him? That is not my approach when I work with clients in my practice. But my father would be different. I am the only one who could save him, my heroic sensibilities insist. And just as quickly I can move into victim mode, overwhelmed by his violent rage.

Neither hero nor victim be. That has become my mantra. And some days I can even pull it off.

My father has resisted saving. Turns out he's never needed to be saved. Just seen. I am slowly learning to do just that, of course, more conveniently and more tragically since he died. Our conversations go much easier these days, although they still tend to revolve around my sons, the weather, and the Steelers new quarterback.

He resisted his assigned therapist after just one session with his therapist. Turns out he couldn't bear going alone so he brought my mother with him. According to fuzzy family memory, the therapist commented that my mother was "bossy" and was part of his problem. She convinced him that the therapist was the problem. I'm sure she convinced him that I was the problem. I know that she believes that, evidenced by her refusal to speak with me.

My father never killed himself. Never with one fell swoop at least. He decided to kill himself slowly over many years.

It is certainly shocking and alarming to hear about my father's thoughts of suicide. I suppose, though, that I would be more surprised if he hadn't tried to kill himself. That would make sense out of the nonsense of the despair that I knew the man to be drowning in.

I know a little of that despair. That's the part that scares me the most. That I have inherited his failed romanticism, his longing to be saved or even to be put out of his misery, to find rest.

Despair. From the Latin and Old French, *de-sperare*. Without hope.

"Hope is a dangerous thing," Morgan Freeman's character Red laments to his friend Andy Dufresne in *Shawshank Redemption*. "Hope can drive a man insane."

"Remember, Red, hope is a good thing, maybe the best thing, and no good thing ever dies," Andy responds.

Hope is complicated. It can be a futuristic phenomenon, robbing the present moment of its power and immediacy. It can be a bypass of harder truths that insist on being reconciled. Yet hope is radical too, a textured and complex memory of the essential goodness of things. Nestled in between the memory of the past and the anticipation of the future.

I hope to be different from my father, better than him. Yet I understand that I am like him; I *am* him in so many ways that all my resistance and efforts at transcendence cannot surmount. I hang precariously between being and the urge to move beyond that being. You become what you behold, it has been said. I have been so obsessed with moving beyond him, clamoring to do things differently, that I have become him in my astute and constant observations of the past, of his past.

I remember. And I hope. Past and future. It seems all-consuming while also whispering of liberation.

I even drafted a 420-page dissertation on the subject. I had pontificated about the subject matter of my dissertation with my advisor during the approval process, insisting on the disembodied scientific merits of my research design with the "troubled youths" who would serve as my subjects and ultimate teachers.

My advisor paused and declared in her perfect Brooklynese, "Don't you know, this is simply about hope."

Simply about hope.

Hope as an antidote to despair.

Or more accurately, a companion to despair. A double helix form of paradox with the imperfect perfection of 10,000 joys and 10,000 sorrows intertwined in our sublime experiences, as Buddhist wisdom reminds us. It is a complicated narrative that resists easy answers and simplistic notions. Nothing to be fixed. No pathology to be treated and resolved in twelve easy, insurance-funded, and evidence-based therapy sessions. Lord knows I've tried.

Innocence must pass through the gauntlet of experience.

The boy must die, not be killed, but die just enough for the man to be made known. If the boy cannot or will not be transformed, then a perpetual adolescence persists. The boy has insatiable needs—to be seen, to be healed, to be rescued. His appetites cannot be satisfied. He longs for power and will stop at nothing to acquire it. As the African proverb extols, the boy who is not embraced by the village, who is not eldered into manhood, will burn the village down to feel its warmth.

The gun had been sold. The bedframe and the headboard where it used to rest had been thrown out in the trash, my mother conspiring to forget her grief away. All that remained was the empty dance floor of a life without her beloved, infuriating but beloved. She longed to lay her head on his shoulder at one last slow dance at one last family wedding at Penn No. 7 Firehall.

That's what I longed for as well: to place my worried head on his chest in a warm embrace between boy and father, to become a man myself. Even if that embrace was alcohol-fueled, the alchemy of Iron City, Winchester Little Cigars, and Old Spice. But I was no longer that boy. He was not my father anymore. And she refused to be my mother, forgetting the son to manage the memory of the father. They were just an amalgam of distant narratives, some of them evolving, some of them stuck in deep hues of amber like a beautiful bug captured in sweet and terrorizing repose.

An instant. A moment. An atom of memory with immense energy and power to be realized in its splitting. That power and that energy are live-giving and potentially lethal all at the same time.

My mother and father—frozen in time on that parquet dance floor in a cleaving but loving embrace. I watched at the periphery with my sword. I wanted to join the dance, my father was looking for the right place to swing his sword.

Never give a sword to a man who has not learned to dance. Dancing helps to nudge the boy into manhood, from innocence to experience. It helps to move soul and spirit into embodiment, into the wonder of muscle and sinew, of bone and marrow, of creaky joints and skin tags, of deeply worn and wonderfully earned grooves in the skin manufactured from delight and sadness alike.

From this sacred dancing, the boy learns to wield the sword of manhood, of the power of the blade that can both wound and protect. Through dancing, the boy learns the difference. And without much fanfare or ecstatic revelation, accidentally but with great resolve and deliberateness, he discovers the manhood that was waiting for him all along.

Chapter Twelve

The greatest tragedy for men in regard to the feminine principle is that their fear alienates them from their own Anima, the principle of relatedness, feeling, and connection to the life force.

James Hollis

She died when I was young, and I don't remember ever meeting her in person, but stories about my grandmother were omni-present, hovering in the ether for my father or mother to pluck down in full mythic mode around the kitchen table or shag-carpeted living room. And this was not a family who easily shared stories or easily uttered a kind word about anyone. But Phyllis Plummer was different. She was a saint if you listened to my father. A savior to my mother, Phyllis, having taken her under her wing as a proxy mother figure, instructing her on the things that my mother's own abusive mother had failed to do. Important things like making chipped corned beef on toast, my father's favorite meal, and how to separate colors from whites when doing laundry. This qualified as sainthood and salvation.

And like all good Irish mothers, she held the tenuous line between sinner and saint, cursing like a sailor and quick with a backhand across my father's and his brother Al's unsuspecting smart mouth. She was a spritely spitfire of a woman, all five-foot-three of her. Her husband towered over her in height, but like most men of his generation, lived in fear of and deference to this dynamo of a woman. My father adored her, I imagine, because she was there to pick up the pieces, literal and figurative, of the messes that my grandfather made when he was drunk. She kept house and took in laundry and seamstress jobs from the neighbors in their Wilkinsburg home, cobbling together a modicum of financial and emotional stability as my grandfather drank away his disability checks.

I only have pictures of her to spark distant and fuzzy memories from my early childhood before she died. She is smiling in all of them, beaming even, resplendent in her cat-eyeglasses, plaid dresses, and grandmotherly shawls over her narrow but powerful shoulders, made hearty from holding up the family. And my father is always glowing when he is captured in the same picture, his arms around her, smiling from ear to ear. The pose is much different than the stoic, stubborn, unsmiling face that he displays in most other family photos.

Phyllis always sported a gold crucifix in those photos, a remnant of her adoration of all things Irish-Catholic, her old lady nylons bunched around her ankles as she knelt on the living room floor fumbling the well-worn rosewood Rosary beads with nicotine-stained fingers, listening to the priests on the radio when her daily chores made her miss Mass that morning. My father always had a Catholic medal around his neck until the day he died, the icon identity toggling between St. Christopher and St. Anthony, patron saints of all things lost, and golden images of a suffering and thorny-crowned Jesus. I inherited the medal he wore throughout his dying process, a bleeding and forlorn Jesus, almost making out the mouthed expression on the medal, "My God, my God, why hast thou forsaken me?" Form follows function, indeed.

I was spared the ravages of Catholic school but went through all the rites at St. Susanna's Parish—Confession, First Communion, and Confirmation. Tuesday nights were for catechism classes, Lenten Fridays were for fried fish sandwiches, and Sundays were for Mass and my father's holy parking strategy to ensure an easy and convenient egress from St. Susanna's parking lot to make it home by kickoff of the Steelers game. There was hell to pay if he got parked in. as he bellowed the name of the

Lord in vain and damned the football-ambivalent crowd to a cold layer of hell.

My father endured his own layer of hell at Catholic school, bearing the misfortune of being a restless and defiant kid in the rigid confines of 1950's painful Catholic pedagogy. Angry nuns commanded the halls and classrooms of St. James School, rulers in hand and spare-the-rod-and-spoil-the-child certitude in their hearts. There was one nun who had it out for my father, his knuckles stained with the bruising from her swift ruler strikes for various offenses. Until my father had had enough.

There are not many stories to be told in my family but this one merited mythic status. As my father liked to brag, Sister Mary-Whatever had it coming to her. She threatened to barrage my father's poor skinned knuckles with another rap of the thick ruler. He warned her not to do it, which obviously just made her attack fiercer. I'm not sure how it actually went down as my father honored his Irish heritage by not letting the truth get in the way of a good story, but he reported that he stood up and punched Sister Mary-Whatever, dropping her like Ali versus Frazier, the Thrilla' in Manilla retooled as the Shame of St. James. It gained him hero status with his classmates but not with the school principal or Jesus for that matter, according to the priests. I bet Jesus got a good laugh out of it, though.

He was summarily expelled and exiled from the Flock, cast out and made to wander the mean streets of Wilkinsburg bearing the sins of this hard-scrabble and hard-drinking generation of men. He didn't wander the requisite forty days in the desert but did hide out at his friend's house for three days, descending into anticipatory hell imagining the punishment and gnashing of teeth that awaited him at the hands of his assuredly disappointed and shamed parents. There would be no resurrection from this shadowy tomb.

Famished and sufficiently full of shame, my father skulked back home, dead man walking he anticipated, as he mounted the stairs of the family's modest walk-up apartment. I can't imagine the kind of dread that crossed the synapses of his young mind, internalizing the notion that he deserved the punishment, believing the messages purported by the nuns, his parents, and an anguished Jesus hanging on the Cross. His family's

God was an Old Testament and OG God, quick to punish, rather than the forgiving Jesus of the Gospel and the lesser-endorsed Beatitudes.

He opened the apartment door as quietly and inconspicuously as he could in the early morning, hoping not to stir his parents from their slumber. Luckily, his father had not come home that night, passed out on a table at the bar. His mother sat in the rocker in the living room, eyes closed, and hands folded around her Rosary, blanket over her lap to cut the cold of the Pittsburgh morning. Here eyes startled open as the creaking door heralded this misguided prodigal son's return. My father stopped in his tracks, frozen with fear.

"Jackie, is that you?" she asked, using the diminutive nickname that only she could call him.

"Yeah, ma," he responded with ears back and eyes cast down like a shamed pet dog.

"Did you punch Sister Mary-Whatever?"

"Yeah, ma," he stuttered and stumbled.

"Did she have it coming to her?"

"Sure did, ma," as the fog of dread lifted in the light of this unexpected shift in interrogation.

She uttered those three magic words that my father longed to hear.

"Good for her…"

They never spoke of it again. Phyllis never told my grandfather about the incident, and he was too drunk most of the time to care anyway.

Sometimes we get surprised by forgiveness. Resurrection happens in the oddest places. Hail Mary passes are hoisted in desperation and occasionally caught for touchdowns, full of Grace. The feminine holds us in full embrace. And we are seduced into adoration.

It's all a little scary for boys stumbling into manhood. This powerful force of the feminine that can both devour and nourish.

Mother Mary comes to us when we find ourselves in trouble, speaking words of wisdom. But sometimes she appears as Kali, severed head, and bloody sword in hand, capable of death and destruction.

We forget that the severed head is that of the demon Raktabija whose blood spawned another demon as each drop descended to the earth. Kali saved the world by severing his head and drinking his blood. We men forget the noble archetypal end of this means of violence, for we imagine that this dark feminine energy may go rogue and come for us. Kali meets Lorena Bobbitt with sundry sharp-edged knives aimed at our imagined fonts of power.

No wonder we men don't know what to do with this powerful image of the feminine that we think exists *out there.* She might want to cuddle, pulling us into her bosom in deep embrace, or she might opt to decapitate us. Either way, the perception is that we are beholden to this powerful force, existing precariously between Life and Death. It scares the demon-spawning blood out of us, and the shit out of us for that matter. Most men exist between the poles of fetishizing the feminine, mounting statues on pedestals to which we can project our longings, or we colonize the feminine, keeping it bound by patriarchy and even burned at the stake when such coven-breaking is called for with our prevailing limited imaginations.

It is often convenient to toggle between the dualist images of women in the dualist Madonna-Whore complex that has existed throughout time. We long for the purity of the virginal mother, she who is without sin, whose blessed womb represents the fertile and untouched land in which our seed can help germinate the coming of the Divine. We, like Joseph, can tolerate our partner's mysterious pregnancy if their only previous sexual partner was God Almighty, him-self. This is the woman we want to bring home to mom, while still longing for the sexual freak in the bedroom—because we like the mystery, we are intrigued by the shadow, we exist on the razor's edge of longing to be consumed. We know somewhere that this dark and mysterious force of the feminine exists within us, but while it is intoxicating to imagine, it also can evoke a fear that is unmanageable and overwhelming as we have little personal structure or cultural models to contain such an evocative energy.

This strange relationship with the feminine can become expressed through our often messy and even violent relationships with women. We insist on access to the mysteries of women as if we are entitled to chip off our piece of the gorgeous and mysterious glacier of the feminine to break into palatable-sized pieces of ice to keep our beer cold. The terrifying trend in projected sexual confusion and the violence it can evoke has been a growing population of "incels"—the involuntary celibates—who feel transgressed by women in their awkward and presumptive attempts at wooing the opposite sex as a means of engaging the force of the Feminine for which they long. The shame of having their advances rebuffed is a rapidly escalating thrust of projected anger. Tragically, one of the primary assertions of manhood in our culture is to grow bigger and angry and full of shadowy, hierarchical power. Men who long for an intimate relationship with the feminine seek that intimacy in the immediate through sex, influenced by the cultural grift of selling the erotic and titular as proxy for authentic intimacy.

As it is classically understood, the rape culture that pervades our culture is about power and the abuse of that power, rather than sex. Short of a healthy relationship with the feminine Force within, men resort to projections of this powerful force onto the unsuspecting women in their various orbits. We saw this dynamic writ large and in technicolor across various new outlets during the Cavanaugh Supreme Court confirmation hearings. The "boys will be boys" ethos has echoed from the locker room to the hallowed halls of the land's highest courts, as memories of Clarence Thomas, Anita Hill, pubic hairs, and Coke cans reverberated from previous hearings of bygone committee-endorsed sexual violence. Witness the underwhelming response to former President Trump's bragging of "grabbing them by the pussy" on the Access Hollywood tapes as mere locker room bravado.

These are merely the highly publicized versions of men's perversions of the relationship with the feminine, as recent statistics terrifyingly report that one in five women have experienced completed or attempted rape in their lifetime, according to the National Sexual Violence Resource Center. And while those statistics of reported rapes and the bevy of unreported sexual assaults and rape are tragic, there are countless episodes of violence that persist between men stumbling toward relationships and women who feel objectified as mere props in satisfying men's sexual appetites as a substitute for engagement with the feminine. So, women withdraw, moving internally and embracing their own power, integrating their own masculine energies, buying their own vibrators, celebrating their autonomy and capacity to move into the world and lead. God is coming back, and, boy, is She *pissed*. Internalized anger wrought over ancestral histories of subjugation and violence and burnings at stakes have moved from hushed whispers in covens and klatches into full-throated, primal screams. And men are terrified as they scramble to hide the knives.

And still, the force of the feminine goes underground. Women are still in danger in the majority of the world. Speaking out and mobilizing politically can bring swift recrimination and even death. The anger that is not spoken embeds in dark places as shame; we as a species can tolerate only so much reality. We resist feeling the dark and powerful force of shame as shame begets exile, exile begets loneliness, and loneliness begets soul death. We practice what psychoanalyst Melanie Klein called projective identification, looking for a place to deposit these unwanted and debilitating emotions instead of feeling them ourselves. The shame gets crumpled up like an unwanted piece of paper and thrown into the closest emotional garbage can, usually our most intimate partners. And the partner picks it up, examines it, and often believes that those unwanted feelings of the partner are actually his own feelings—"Wait, maybe I have reason to be ashamed." The term *gaslighting*, a form of this projective identification, has made it into the cultural zeitgeist and collective vocabulary.

And in this scenario, men do not want to feel the shame either. We as a culture as a whole do not metabolize or integrate our shame particularly well, especially men. Men's shame and the abject grief that it can evoke are usually funneled into culturally accepted and reified anger and even rage. We are allowed and even encouraged to be angry, but shame is unacceptable to admit so it finds purchase within our bodies and souls, wreaking havoc.

For men of a certain age, we remember the kitschy TV series, The Incredible Hulk, with thin and wiry Bill Bixby as Dr. Bruce Banner and behemoth Lou Ferrigno as The Hulk. Banner would show up in a random town to right a wrong or an injustice, while unwittingly transformed into the Hyde-like character of The Hulk, clothes tattered as he grew larger in his rage. The wrong would be righted, but not without the shrapnel of his anger leaving a path of destruction and chaos like a nail bomb filled with screws and nail heads and bolts and other pieces of metal cobbled together from the scraps of our souls. Dr. Banner worked to keep his rage at bay but knew the inevitability of its expression. "Don't make me angry," he would warn, "You wouldn't like me when I'm angry." We men know our rage, are terrified of it, and are still seduced by the power and the effect it has on those around us. But it isolates men, removing us from the very relational capacity we long for. At the end of each show, the camera would pan to Banner leaving the town, rucksack slung sadly over his shoulder, walking towards the next town in complete isolation and loneliness as the melancholic piano theme played him off the stage and television screen.

Men become angry and even rageful to suppress the force of the feminine but paradoxically, elevate the feminine upon a pedestal to be worshipped and venerated. This dynamic can be extrapolated to the typical cycle of abusive relationships that have pervaded our history—men become violent towards their partners as a means of subjugating them and then turn to hold these same partners in loving embrace, assuring them that "it won't ever happen again" or "I promise I'll make it up to you." We long for encounter with the feminine so we worship our partners, our mothers, as proxy for the Great Mother.

We fumble over ourselves in mating rituals, strutting around with colorful feathers held high, or we fight one another like chimpanzees to assure our potential mates that we are stronger and fiercer. We have become obsessed with making money as a demonstration of our largesse, showing off larger cars and other fancy wares as a testament to our potential as an adequate provider. Battles rage to build the tallest skyscraper or amass the most wealth, to become the ultimate winner, and to the victor go the spoils. We delight in the pride of our sexual prowess, the ability to bring our partners to climax as a goal to be met or box to be checked, spawning industries of pills, lotions, and potions to make our dicks harder and our partners more satisfied. All of this Big Dick Energy as yet another means of proving our worth.

Our worth.

Love me. Don't leave me. Without these external markers of triumphalism, we are left to our own devices. Without this externalized dance with the feminine, we are subject to our own realities. That we bear shame, bear grief, that we long for connection. That we are alone. That we will die. That the Mother, the Universe may not be so benevolent after all. The revelation can be terrorizing.

And our partners become achingly confused with this bipolar emotional dance. They resist our anger, proclaiming that they will no longer be held hostage to the violence that men have visited upon women, and other men for that matter, for ages. Cultural models of solidarity arise, as women dare to stand together against the personal and cultural violence of suppression and subjugation. While many other women still exist in dangerous situations, balanced between life and death at the hands and fists of violent partners.

Our partners also resist our adoration, as they become more aware that worship is not necessarily about them as living, breathing, multi-dimensional beings; rather, they are merely the receptacles of our projections about the feminine. They do not feel seen, they exist as props for the unfolding drama of relationship with the idealized version of the Mother. Women in my therapy practice have grown weary of these regressive tendencies, imagining that their partners move through the world as one more needy child to care for in the family brood, tugging at their dress for attention.

We long to maintain connection with the Mother, to proffer ourselves before the great altar of the feminine. We cycle through proving and performing, to assuage the fear and shame that lie just below the surface of our bravado. Men suffer the recapitulation of separation from the Mother over and over again, reminded of the certainty of separation and taken to its ultimate expression, the slow and inevitable descent into death. We are reminded of our fundamental disconnection from the life force, as opposed to women, who bear the potential of creating, sustaining, and fomenting life through childbirth. Even those women who chose or cannot have children are reminded of the potential for life and the connection with the cycles of Nature through their own monthly menses cycles.

Men exist within their own orbits, seeking an exit velocity beyond the pull of mortality. The myth of Narcissus reminds us that we gaze upon the image of our own constructed beauty in the reflecting pool, feasting upon the expense of everything else around us until we are consumed and drown. Like Narcissus, we are born from gods, but we are fallible, we are subject to death. Even that understanding of our mortality is insufficient to break our attentive and adoring gaze. We serve ourselves while longing for a connection to something more expansive than ourselves, trapped in this liminal space until the throes of midlife, or failed marriages, or dreams deferred wake us up. And the vacuum that is created, the evolving sense of malaise and dissatisfaction, must be filled, as nature abhors a vacuum. And so, the pattern repeats itself—we roll that heavy boulder up the hill in fine Sisyphean fashion, only to have it roll back down the hill once again, to the very beginning of our labor.

And yet, that constancy of cycling through rolling and re-rolling that same boulder may provide the answers that we seek, the satisfaction and filling of that void that we sometimes acknowledge with a deeper consciousness. But the answer is not particularly sexy. The answer may be the cycle itself, the rolling and re-rolling of that boulder, as inane and repetitive as it might seem. We are all participating in and subject to the cycles of Nature, despite all of our best efforts to tame or master the forces of Nature, whom we adorn with the name Mother. Through all of our striving, proving, and performing, we discover that these efforts are for naught. Hedge fund accounts grow, political power is amassed and monetized, statues are constructed in adoration, penthouse toilets are adorned in gold, and it all amounts to—nothing. Markets tank, election cycles turn on the whims of a manipulated electorate, statues are toppled in populist revolt, and even gold tarnishes.

This rant is not meant to fetishize poverty or to advocate an inert existence without accomplishment or striving for creativity. It's a good ride while flush with cash and currying the favor of social media followers through our cultural currency of fame. And creativity is the ultimate act of liberation toward the fullest essence of ourselves. But we must be privy to the notion that we are in a constant relationship with the other, with the Other. We are in a radical interconnectedness with all that is—with the immanent of the other in all of the sublime banality of day to day to relationships and to the transcendent Other, the Divine Mother, the Holy Father, the Great Spirit, even the nameless, faceless Void.

This is the one translation of the embrace of the feminine character that men long for in quiet and even desperate moments of repose and reflection but fear as soft or even "gay." In certain circles, if we dare to express the desire to connect, then we will be perceived of as "weak." Weakness is tantamount to death in our culture of masculinity, as the culture tends to exile anything that is outside the purview of an accepted and reified expression of what it means to be a man. And exile is death, set apart from the community, subject to ridicule, bullying, and alienation. Note the backlash toward alternative models of masculinity being proposed, as podcasters and pundits alike participate in the "fuck your feelings" ethos while advocating for men to return to being the triumphal master of family systems, tyrannical political overseers, and bullying titans of business practices without regulation. In moments of cultural change, those in power will cling to old models and yearn for a return to bygone colonial and repressive models of masculinity. Gatekeeping forces can become desperate and schizoid when their power is questioned and threatened. New cultural models that approximate equality will appear oppressive to archaic models of masculinity.

The longing for power without consideration of its effects is a fundamentally adolescent trope. Fittingly, our young men aspire for something greater than themselves, be it participating in group structures such as sports teams, garage bands, or even the military. For most, the prevailing model of this larger "other" devolves into the corporate model, as the quest for power is translated into the pursuit of money and fame—reified and reinforced by men in power serving inadequately as pseudo-Elders. There is an expanding nexus of political power, religious zeal, and financial prowess that is marketed as the logical and reasonable end that justifies all sorts of oppressive and even fascist-adjacent means. And our young men gobble it up like pablum, convinced that it is manna from Heaven. The Hero no longer saves the day or rights the wrong; rather, he amasses stockpiles of gold and stock options, and consumes all resources in service of those hoarding habits. Everything appears as a commodity to be used and abused, from natural resources to human ones, all of it kindling for the fire that we stoke to keep the cold night and the monsters lurking in its dark at bay. Those fires, large, consumptive, and inefficient, initially blaze fiercely but are not sustainable. They will not keep us warm; instead they will consume everything around us as they rage beyond the paltry firebreaks we desperately dig in full retreat.

Most cultures world-wide and throughout history have prescribed an antidote for this understandable yet immature yearning for power to which our young men aspire. The young man has often required an unsubtle and often disruptive participation in a Rite of Passage, a deliberate ritual in which the young man crosses the threshold into adulthood as a means of understanding that they are participating not only in their own personal narratives but are subjects in a larger narrative far greater than themselves. The natural fires of pursuing power are tempered and held by the community container of Elders who themselves have moved beyond the trappings of adolescence into authentic wisdom.

Through trial and ritualized encounters with the inevitable force of death, the young man understands and is humbled by his finitude. He can then return to the community in this sublime paradox of largesse and smallness, of invincibility and humility, of infinity and bound by death. His continuing unfolding into an authentic Self can then be in service of something larger than himself, what was once understood as chivalry. Not merely holding car doors open on date night or helping little old ladies across the street; rather, a harnessing of masculine energy in service of something noble and true, of a larger narrative that is good and just.

This is not a hierarchical phenomenon in which the maturing young man abdicates or sacrifices his identity to feed a larger, consuming beast. This is the model espoused by most of our culture, be it corporate or militaristic, or more personally, to appease violent fathers hellbent on keeping their powerful sons at bay. This is a model based in holarchy, as the young man matures into an evolving expression of his fullest identity which then becomes in service of something larger while maintaining that identity. You can imagine a set of Russian nesting dolls in which each smaller doll is embedded into the larger doll while bearing the same form as both the smaller and larger dolls on either end. Or more poetically, each drop in the ocean maintains its individual identity while also being part of the larger, expansive Ocean. We are not a drop in the ocean—we are the entire ocean in a drop as Rumi reminds us. Individual cells coalesce into larger organ systems, all of which combine to constitute this wonderful meatsuit we call a body.

The antidote to the prolonged adolescence that ravages our halls of power demands a certain element of leadership that has been lacking until the more recent dissatisfaction with old models of masculinity and an awakening of new and revolutionizing ways of being a man. There is a growing population of men who are doing the work to move into true Elderhood, to model these new ways of being a man that are both fierce and compassionate. We are compelled to tend to our own souls first, as most of us missed out on ritualizing our transition into adulthood through community-based rites of passage. The Hero's Journey is a young man's game of ascent, while moving into Elderhood is primarily a journey of descent into the dark, moist, and terrorizing yet forgiving fecundity. It is a return to Mother, of the earth rather than of the spirit.

It is burying our fathers in the Sacred Earth with grace and forgiveness, with grief and wonder, with their dogs or in whatever way they have seen fit, in their births, their deaths, and their re-births.

My father was a mutterer.

I would catch him at the kitchen table, in the cinder block basement putting together his military models in the corner, or just walking around the house with strange, indecipherable incantations on his lips.

If I listened more closely, it was mostly about what my mother had done to him or things she hadn't done that irked him to no end. It was as if he offered his first fruits to her and that she had refused him, evoking shame and ultimately anger.

Like so many of our relationships, theirs was bound by trauma bonding—my father, having adored and been adored by his mother, longed for similar tenderness from his wife. She, having never known her biological father, sexually abused by her stepfather, and knocked up by her first husband many years her senior, knew only shame when it came to men. My father would long to please her to receive her blessing. My mother would withhold it just long enough and strident enough to project her shame onto him, while seducing him to come back for more. It was an odd way to grow up and observe their relational dynamics, especially when their vitriol for one another would unite in a confluence of violence towards me in equal parts hatred and what approximated love.

I too often catch myself muttering also. Muttering about my wife, about all of the injustices she has visited upon me, how underappreciated I am, and certainly how undersexed. And it terrifies me. To the inevitable repetition of my father's patterns, to have my relationship with my wife a re-capitulation of my own and my ancestors' working out of all of our individual and collective traumas. And in concert—sometimes resonant, sometimes dissonant—with her traumas. And yet there's so much more to this story than our partnering traumas. I can shake it off at times and realize that my muttering and my dissatisfaction have nothing to do with my wife, she in her brilliance and beauty, her stubbornness and pride. It has everything to do with my own projections on to her, my lofty expectations tugging at her sleeve for her to be both wife and mother, to embody what I desire from the force of the feminine. I can be equal parts performative and resentful at times. I bemoan the dance that we do with one another, yet like my father, I return for more. It is all I know when I am in the fog of unknowing, unconsciously repeating these ineffectual but familiar patterns.

We all walk around in this state of confusion born from this emotional hand-to-hand, soul-to-soul combat. All of us dissatisfied or at least nonplussed. Especially as the bedrock of institutions, including old concepts of marriage, crumble around us while something new is waiting to be born. How did we get here, and how do we get back? Not back to the banality of rusty, antiquated sex roles, but back to a memory of authentic relationships, intimacy, and encounters for which most of us long. A memory of the future. To come home and recognize it for the first time. All of it paradoxical. The most balanced and reasonable, and even paradoxical, explanation of love that I have heard comes from the poet Ranier Marie Rilke, "Love consists of this: two solitudes that meet, protect, and greet one another."

This solitude for men is not merely the stoic, lone wolf resplendent in cowboy movies of lore, nor is it the needy, domesticated Labrador always at the heels of his owner looking for heavy petting. We are afraid of being too independent, too alone, and yet we also fear domestication and dependency. This is the wounding of the masculine that we rarely acknowledge, especially in the company of other men, preferring to discuss our portfolios or Monday morning quarterback that Sunday's football games. As James Hollis so wonderfully expressed in *Under Saturn's Shadow: The Wounding and Healing of Men*, "When men feel the wound that cannot heal, they either bury themselves in a woman's arms and ask her for healing, which she *cannot* provide, or they hide themselves in macho pride and enforced loneliness."

There is a third option between these harrowing poles: the force of the feminine lies within all men, what Carl Jung called the force of the Anima which resides deeply protean and often ignored in the soul. Just as women contain the balancing masculine force of the Animas that is becoming increasingly integrated as women re-discover their inherent power. It has been suggested, often in a cursory and deeply dissatisfying way, that men should "embrace their feminine side." This is often code to implore men to become quiescent, in service to the military warlords or corporate overseers that rely on blind allegiance to maintain corrupt power structures. The simplistic notion is often met with bombastic resistance, demanding men resume their "rightful" places as the conquering head of the household and head of industry, a return to the fantasy of a Great America that relied on subjugation, colonialism, and commodification of resources— of products and peoples.

It is easy to bemoan the perceived struggles of the white, cis-gendered, American man, as if he and we deserve whatever comeuppance and shame that is thrust upon us as a rightful penance, if not punishment for a few thousand years of bad behavior. And it may be so. Yet it robs the culture; it robs our young men yearning for Elders and models of what a righteous and just masculinity might look like. It is remarkably easy then for men to fall into the pseudo-narrative of being hero or victim. Men cling to the notion of their own heroism, but a shadowy hero who is hellbent on destruction and vanquishing and perceived threats with increasingly delusional paranoia. Or he becomes the perpetually maligned victim, ineffectual and inert, unable to muster the fierceness that the world so desperately demands in this time of social upheaval and environmental havoc.

We men are trapped in these unimaginative old models without tools or Elders to create sustainable change beyond the fundamentalism of archaic gender roles that have been reified over years of destruction and death. Still, there is a way out, a way through. Men can, and are, endeavoring to integrate masculine and feminine forces within themselves. This is the sacred marriage that poets, sages, and alchemists have espoused for years. The alchemists have spoken about the *coninuctio oppositorum*, the combining of two opposite substances or essences, even ideas, into a unity greater than the sum of its parts. Mythopoetic writer and therapist Marion Woodman has assured us that the entire process of the soul's journey is toward the inner marriage of the mature masculine and the mature feminine. Because of its potential for creating change, it is not surprising that such a radical and paradoxical unitive vision did not make it into the canon, but the non-canonical Gospel of Thomas describes it this way:

> When and if you make all twos into one:
> If you make the side you show
> Like the side you hide, and
> The side inside like the side outside
> And your higher side like your lower one
> With the result that you make
> The man and woman in you as one
> So that there is nothing more to
> Become either male or female;
> When you find what really sees—
> Eyes in the place of your physical eye—
> And you find what really grasps,
> And stands, and walks;
> When you make your self-image
> The original image of humanity;
> Then you will be entering
> The original guiding power,
> The king- and queendom
> Of the Holy One.

The original guiding power. A unity greater than the sum of its parts. It is a return to what has always been, while also being radically new. New wine cannot be stored in old wineskins. They cannot bear the profundity, and they burst. Men need not fear this dissolution, loss of identity, or a slippery descent into softness or subjugation. There is a possibility for a full and effective expression of fierceness in the service of noble movements, and of of righteous causes that demand the integrated man, able to hold the hard edge of the mature masculine balanced with the radical relatedness of the mature feminine. We are doomed without it. We are doomed to bear the violence and dis-integration of a world wrought by men stuck in silly adolescent cycles of narcissistic lust for power or men who have moved into de-animation, afraid to exert their power at all. Our world suffers. And our men suffer. Our sons suffer. They and we are denied our full birthright as integrated, unique, and powerful expressions of the Divine—capable of creativity and justice, of journeying and coming home, and ultimately capable of restoring and renewing our souls and the *anima mundi*, the soul of the world.

When the mature and integrated feminine meets the mature and integrated masculine, life bursts through the veil, and we delight in the hopeful possibility. As radical and subversive theologian Matthew Fox reminds us, "From the healthy union of feminine and masculine is born a living child. A mystical child. One in love with the universe, in love with life." The fruit of this labor need not be an actual child, as it is just as life-giving to birth an idea, to birth a different way of being, to birth a different kind of masculinity.

My third son Arlo was born from an evolving integration of masculine and feminine forces. And there is ease that transpires, a flow of sorts that is a testament to the faculty and potentiality of pursuing integration. He arrived gently in the predawn morning of a cold New Mexico winter darkness. My first son struggled through his posterior positioning and the excruciating pain it caused his mother. My second son was born into warm, welcoming waters at home, but not before he reconsidered the whole project, returning to the safe confines of his mother's womb before conceding to being born. Arlo was born with a remarkable lightness as his mother had prepared for the birth through her own integration of mature masculine and feminine forces. Fathers who are deliberate in their own efforts at integration can hold the container for the work of birthing, equal parts fierce and tender.

My wife labored mostly by herself, free from the expectations of the expectant father and interventions from the lovely, attentive midwife at her side, almost feral and animal-like. The whole process was a gift to me, a gift to our son, a gift to the world. Like all of our boys. Living children. Mystical children.

Arlo has grown into a remarkable young man, curly haired, earnest, and feral himself. In love with the world. Still a teenager consumed with teenager things behind slammed bedroom doors and in front of video game consoles. But so fully himself, or at least as much as possible given the expected trappings of adolescence in this culture and in our home.

And his is the continued legacy of son to his father. Of his father to his grandfather. Of all of us to the Great Father. Bearing the same ancestral woundings and bearing the same possibility for healing from these woundings. For the power of healing is our birthright, a conduit to the universal yet unique expression of the Divine. This Kingdom, this Queendom, as the Gospel writer Thomas assures us, is here among us.

And waiting for us.

Chapter Thirteen

Today we need heroes of descent, not masters of denial, mentors of maturity who can carry sadness, who give love to aging, who show soul without irony or embarrassment.

James Hillman

I followed the deer past the naked trees nestled together in tight formation against the coming harsh cold of winter, passing behind the Pasqualino's, the Lynch's, the Gazzo's, the Maguire's, the DeFazio's, and the other working-class bastions of Pittsburgh ethnic swath. The deer casually crossed the road to a well-worn path, more recently tread by their hooves, while also holding the memory of the feet of any number of neighborhood children climbing the small hill to the field over the years.

We were literal kids, I suppose. There were the Big Kids, the group of long-haired adolescents that held court in our neighborhood, slipping off into the woods to swill beer or take hits of makeshift toilet-paper roll bongs. And we were the Little Kids, often trailing at their heels in hopes of learning the norms of sex, drugs, and rock n' roll, risking a torturous taunt about our acne or glasses or shaved head or a half-empty Iron City beer can thrown at our heads.

And there was the field, a small, flat, patch of grass and dirt that perched at the confluence of two massively steep streets, Clay Drive and

Key Drive, and the level Bryant Drive. It served as a place of escape and also an expression of adolescent hubris, hosting neighborhood skirmishes of whatever sport was in season. It brought the community together, as neighborhood clean-up parties were organized when grass needed to be mowed or weeds pulled, or rusting baseball backstops needed to be replaced. Our fathers would schlep their lawnmowers and picks and shovels up to the field, then stand around drinking beer while directing the kids to perform their labor.

As I made my way up the serpentine path to the field, trailing the deer at a sufficient distance to learn the new neighborhood norms, I was surprised at how overgrown the area had become with oak, sycamore and buckeye trees and saplings vying for space and waning sunlight. The neighborhood had once re-cycled quickly with a new crop of kids growing quickly to replace the teenagers moving reluctantly into the workforce and banal adulthood. Families entrenched from bygone and mostly European and Catholic immigration waves swore fidelity to the Pope's edicts against birth control, supplying their own form of social capital. The neighborhood now mostly consisted of aging stalwarts like my mother or childless couples settled in their affordable first homes, all uninterested in keeping the field in prime playing form.

It was also remarkable how the dimensions of the field took on a more immediate and pragmatic scale in my adulthood, as my lungs heaved in the frigid air, and my knees ached from climbing the hills that I once flew over with delight and a full supply of joint cartilage. Eddie Vorpagel's fence served as the right field wall, in what seemed a clout of Babe Ruth or at least Willie Stargell proportion to clear the fence for a homer. Now, as I stood silent at the missing home plate in front of the decaying boards and wire of a rusting backstop, I realized that it couldn't have been more than 150 feet down the line.

It's funny how certain things seem so much smaller than you remember. And other things still loom so large.

As I looked around the landscape of this holy ground, I failed to find any trace of my escort deer friends. All hopes for my idealized vision quest were dashed by the absence of spirit animals…there would, sadly, be no Dances With Deer this time around. I wiped away sweat from my brow and chuckled at myself, at the romantic delusions of a youth spent escaping from the ravages of family life, at matinees in dark theaters on hot, muggy summer days, the bored teenager box office employee affording me passage into taboo R-rated films at my tender age. I lived a lifetime, many lifetimes, in front of multiplex screens; I killed the shark, I got the girl, I took lives, I saved lives, and they saved mine.

I stumbled over an old, exposed root at the edge of the field, barely keeping my balance, when I saw him. He was a noble and elegant creature, a huge buck with ten points, the kind of animal that my father and his buddies salivated over with Ahab zeal. He raised his head and twitched his tail, unimpressed with my nostalgia, then slowly began ambling toward the edge of the field. I followed with no expectations, my mind was still silent for once and free from obsessive thoughts, magical thinking, and imagined reverie.

The buck was even more impressive as I inched closer. He did not startle; rather, just lifted his head from his foraging to acknowledge my presence and move on to his next station. I paused when he paused. As I waited for his next move, I was consumed once again by a torrent of memories, of sneaking into the Big Kids Camp to sift through the rubble of their campfires, hoping to find a swig of warm beer at the bottom of a discarded Iron City can or piece together the tattered pages of a Playboy or Hustler magazine to catch fleeting sight of a boob or pussy.

I was entranced. The rhythm of stops and starts proceeded for what seemed like both an instant and an eternity as we both made our way into the woods. I passed the old spaceship log where my friends and I acted scenes and fantasies of space travel from Lost in Space and Star Trek. We all longed to boldly go where no man had gone before. And secretly, we all longed to be anywhere except in our homes and their maddening alchemy of liquor, cigarette smoke and shame. It was the same myth told over and over again throughout the ages, the young man who is compelled to go on a journey in search of the Grail to save the wounded Grail King and restore the Kingdom. And participate in danger, even cheating death along the way. And to lie in the warm beds of welcoming women—seeking comfort, release and to piece together the lost remnants of the divine feminine in our own souls.

And yet there was an odd comfort to this life. There existed a semblance of predictability and ordinary that settled in the marrow of our bones, of our fathers' bones. The spirit of home that clung to the surface area of every crag and crevice of my father's ashes that rested inside the box inside my jacket pocket, so close to my heart. And a million miles away.

This is the particular tension of this accidental manhood I had stumbled into, the comforts of home, stability, and redemption juxtaposed with the longing for adventure, for thrill, for the wildness of the road. Long suppressed by the conventions of culture, it seems to express itself from the shadowy, chthonic realm in stereotypical purchases of convertibles and motorcycles and mid-life affairs or, at the very least, sublimation into the dogmas of money and status and triumphal pursuits of power and political and religious certitude.

Rainer Maria Rilke captures the essence of the tension so remarkably well:

Sometimes a man stands up during supper and walks outdoors,
and keeps on walking, because of a church that stands somewhere
in the East.

And his children say blessings on him
as if he were dead.

And another man, who remains inside his own house,
stays there, inside the dishes and in the glasses,

so that his children have to go far out into the world,
towards that same church,

which he forgot.

My father longed for the wild, surrounding himself with images of the fantasy, Native American t-shirts and figurines of wolves and bears and large-antlered bucks, while he remained inside his own house, inside empty beer cans, whiskey bottles and full ashtrays of discarded cigarette butts. But I don't really blame him anymore; I just don't think he knew any better. I don't think he had any real models, having to settle for two-dimensional men like his hero John Wayne or fabricated, romanticized stories of war and heroism that persisted as thin veneer over the corporatized war machine. He couldn't possibly allow himself to feel the disappointment, the furor, the tragedy of being caught up in the cultural trappings of the distorted masculine.

So, he created targets for his displaced anger and rage and disappointment. Gays. The "colored" who were moving into his town. The "Suits" who worked in air-conditioned offices above his hot factory floor. The unions who dared to fight for his protection. Nixon. Hippies. It was the typical, bigoted roll call for the disgruntled and disappointed late twentieth century man that persists into our own time and our own culture.

And often times, that list included me too.

James Baldwin was speaking of a considerable number of different things when he said, "I imagine one of the reasons people cling to their hates too stubbornly is because they sense, once hate is gone, they will be forced to deal with the pain." But he could have easily been talking about my father as well.

These thoughts coursed through my head in swirling anxiety—the dizziness of freedom as Kierkegaard describes it. I looked up through tired but clear eyes to find the buck had disappeared, leaving me alone in my thoughts and insights and even my complicated version of forgiveness.

I clambered through the edge of the forest to the manicured edges of backyard lawns, standing just above the hill behind the Antonucci's house, a vantage point from where I could see my old house. It looked different now, smaller, and almost sad in that it contained smallness. And yet it looked more familiar and comforting to me than ever. It seemed as if I was examining it under a microscope, the details and crags of the red bricks and shingled roof, while also viewing it from a million miles away in deep and quiet space. It was the place of home for which I had longed. The place of forgiveness. The place of love.

This thing we call love, the term bandied about in our everyday lexicon, often carelessly, like how we "love" tacos or about our hallowed freedoms, "America—love it or leave it." Within our expression of love, there remains a consistent and aching longing for something, somewhere, a place or a state of ease. In this blessed state, our minds settle into sweet repose, liberated from the tyranny of reason and regret. The tiresome effort of propping up our perceived Self, with all its contingent and confusing demands and hurts and resentments and even celebrated accomplishments, is cast aside. Our souls are free to roam unencumbered by the demands of performance and the discordant dance of our individual ego expression, the catastrophic fallacy of the Western ideal of the rugged individualist.

We stand naked, trembling but unafraid, in a sublime collision with the Real, with all that is. And we allow ourselves the full purchase of wonder and awe, of the suffering and the violence, of the luminous beauty of both shadow and light. We stand or kneel or crawl before our God, or gods, or family, or spouse, or silent darkness, or mostly before our very Self in sacred encounter. We bear our skin tags and stretch marks, our scars and wrinkles, a middle-aged gut and back hair, elderly forgetfulness, the sublime certitude of adolescent zeal. All of it.

This is the unique and brilliant expression of the Divine that each of us bears in a deep place of silence and unknowing. Buddhists, in the soulful playfulness of koan, ask, "What was your face before it was born?" Sufis describe it within the continuum of *fana* and *baqa*: fana, where there is an abdication of the perceived self in the presence of God and baqa, where one is able to retain an awareness of the true self while being fully aware of the Divine presence simultaneously. Christian holy writ frames it in a surrender of self to the crucified Christ, "I have been crucified with Christ. It is no longer I who live, but Christ who lives in me." (Galatians 2:20, ESV).

Those intellectual ideas can be intriguing and formative angels to wrestle with, but even as I write the words, I can feel the drift of the strong current of thought and reason pulling me further and further from shore. From the place of being, from the pull of gravity that holds my feet to this sacred ground of planetary rock, as it spins in place and catapults around the sun, spiraling through the universe.

This is the place to which we long to return. The place of belonging, liberated from the alienation from whatever it is we deem to be larger than our own self-identity: God, god(s), the Ground of Being, the Universe, the Fates, even.

This is the great lie—somehow, we convince ourselves that we are separate. Modern culture doesn't help the process of belonging much, coaxing, and cajoling us in ways obvious and subtle that we aren't enough. The violence to be found within the confines of this fallacy can be overwhelming, and we have demonstrated remarkably creative ways of veiling, sublimating, coursing along the way of spiritual bypass and positivism, or medicating our way out of this space of dissonance.

And others of us rest in the sadness of this space of estrangement, delighted to relish our roles as victims of a larger force—our families of origin and their attached narratives of trauma, a vengeful God, or even Big Government, intent on absconding with our personal liberties and freedoms.

This entire continuum of identity, victim, or conqueror reflects a false innocence, as if we were still orphaned children, modern-day Horatio Alger's with sufficiently long bootstraps, or conversely those of us who bask in the glow of racial, financial, or circumstantial privilege without admission of gratitude or accountability. Others of us cling to the notion of religious triumphalism, as if we have earned our innocence through God's favor, or at least having been born in the right school district. Religious charlatans prey on our collective false innocence, assuring us that we can name and claim our blessedness, usually while increasing theirs.

Simone Weil assured us that "false gods transform suffering into violence, while true gods transform violence into suffering." We are not comfortable with the notion of suffering, and our sadistic projection of the pain that it often evokes onto others and the masochistic internalization of that pain onto ourselves is equally and reprehensibly violent. The earned innocence, that translation of our violence into suffering, only comes through experience, bearing the enormous task and responsibility of crossing the threshold from innocent child to experienced adult and eventually to the wisdom of elder.

And this is the great paradox: we are already home, but we must leave home to discover that elusive truth. We have to bear the separation of the journey to understand the grace of returning home, of never having been separated from that place of belonging and identity. "For whoever would save his live will lose, but whoever loses his life for my sake will save it," Jesus has reminded us. This is the essence of the definition of suffering, to participate in the pathos of existence and truly restore and renew that innocence for which we long. The essence of the pathos of that experience of the suffering contained in the reality of our existence, is contained in the word "compassion," literally to "suffer with." Remarkably, one of the translations into the English word compassion is derived from the Hebrew, *rachamim*, which means to be enwombed. It is the love of a mother for her child, one without boundaries, in which the mother intuitively understands that the child is both of her essence while also being entirely separate and "other" from her.

God as Father, who inspires the journey.

God as Mother, who welcomes you back home.

I pulled the box of his ashes from inside of my coat, opening the plastic bag from inside the silver box to feel the crags and sharp edges of his long-burned body. It wasn't him anymore, but I could feel his true presence, even his spirit, so strongly now. And I sensed that he was part of the bones of the antlers atop the noble head of the buck in the field, its marrow running fierce during this season of rutting, when male deer seek out females to continue their line. When they are also most susceptible to being hunted. And in the coming months, he could be found in the discarded antlers on the cold, hard, unforgiving ground, portending echoes of the hooves of fawn and doe to be born in spring.

The gray dust slipped through my fingers back into the bag. I sealed it and placed it back in the box, closing my coat against the raw cold. I slipped carefully down the side of the house, so as not to arouse suspicion from Mrs. Antonucci peeking out from behind her living room drapes in vigilant neighborhood watch. I crossed the street, pausing at the entrance of my old driveway, stepping carefully over the various trash and other objects of backfill accumulated over the years in attempts to extend the backyard, making my way down the small, uneven hill to my father's final place of rest.

I realized that I had returned to this place of history and knowing, while also in this unique and unknowable time. My journey had taken me to this place of restoration, to an unexpected place of solace, of an accidental manhood. It was the end of one journey and the beginning of another.

And my father was with me. I had become so familiar with his absence, or at least the perceived absence. He had always been with me; he had always shown up and always persisted. It was often rageful, other times steely silent, but this newly discovered presence as guardian and oddly revered ancestor was equal parts disorienting and comforting. The memories, once thought impenetrable and intractable, had somehow been transformed. I had been transformed as son and as father. And I hope my father has been transformed.

I join my own story with the story of my father—and generations of Herzog ancestors—and those still unfolding with my boys. All of these disparate narratives somehow come together, stubbornly at times, into The Story, the universal narrative that has always been and will persist, the echo of poets and bards, prophets and priests, and all story tellers throughout time. The story echoes the ultimate archetypal expression of the journey towards the restoration of the Kingdom, Parsifal, and the Grail King, as the King reminds the earnest, wayfaring boy,

> Be forewarned,
> Behind the quest burns
> Aspiration.
> A yearning for the heights
> So intense,
> That ultimate failure
> Even death itself
> Though risked,
> Is no obstacle.
>
> And as well,
> You must come to know
> Indeed, must embrace,
> The deepest, moist sorrow
> Of your heart.

Fire and water,
The marriage of yearning and sorrow
Gives birth to the quest.

I kicked a heel into the blade of the shovel, and it sliced through the hard clay after a few attempts.
I buried my father with the dogs. And returned home.

Made in the USA
Coppell, TX
03 May 2024

31966392R00111